MW01122428

Criminal Justice
Recent Scholarship

Edited by
Marilyn McShane and Frank P. Williams III

A Series from LFB Scholarly

Police Taser Utilization
The Effect of Policy Change

Michael E. Miller

LFB Scholarly Publishing LLC
El Paso 2010

Library of Congress Cataloging-in-Publication Data

Miller, Michael E.
  Police taser utilization : the effect of policy change / Michael E.
Miller.
    p. cm. -- (Criminal justice : recent scholarship)
  Includes bibliographical references and index.
  ISBN 978-1-59332-389-9 (hardcover : alk. paper)
  1. Police--United States--Attitudes. 2. Stun guns--United States. 3.
Police brutality--United States. I. Title.
  HV8141.M48 2010
  363.2'32--dc22

                                        2010012812

ISBN 978-1-59332-389-9

Printed on acid-free 250-year-life paper.

Manufactured in the United States of America.

Table of Contents

List of Tables

List of Figures

List of Acronyms and Abbreviations

ASP   An expandable metal baton is an impact weapon used to deliver blows to specific areas of the body to gain compliance from a resisting or noncompliant suspect. This weapon is issued by the Orlando Police Department.

CED   Conducted energy devices encompass a wide range of weapons that rely on electrical shock to incapacitate combative and/or noncompliant suspects. These include stun guns, stun belts, electronic control devices, and tasers.

CEW   Conducted Electrical Weapon is another term used to a wide range of weapons that rely on electrical shock to incapacitate combative and/or noncompliant suspects. These include stun guns, stun belts, electronic control devices, and tasers.

CN   Chloroacetaphenone, or tear gas, was introduced for police use in the 1960s. Its principle use was in civil disorders or riots. It is an irritant that produces burning in the eyes, nose, and throat.

CS   Ortho/Chlorobenzal-Malononitrile is another disabling gas. It came into use during the 1960s and 1970s. CS gas causes pain in the nose, throat, and chest.

ECD   Electronic control device is a term used by the Orlando Police Department to describe the taser in their policies and procedures.

LTL   Less-than-lethal weapons are a category of use-of-force weapons, which are designed to gain compliance from noncompliant subjects without inflicting serious or lethal injuries.

OC   Oleoresin Capsicum, or OC, is derived from an irritant in cayenne pepper. It is a bottle propelled by compressed air that is sprayed into the facial area of a noncompliant subject. This results in mild respiratory distress and temporary loss of vision.

Acknowledgments

This project could have been completed without the help and support of many people. First and foremost, I could not have completed it without the love and support of my family and friends. The data collection for the project could not have been completed without the help and support of the Orlando Police Department. I am grateful to Chief Michael McCoy who gave me his approval and provided me access to data and personnel for the project. Captain Jeff Goltz, PhD., was my agency contact and provided invaluable assistance and advice. I also wish to express my thanks to my advisors, Dr. Steve Holmes, Dr. Sophia Dziegielewski, Dr. Eugene Paoline, and Dr. Mark Lanier from the University of Central Florida. I am very grateful for your contributions.

Taser Use By Police: A Continuing Controversy

The issue of police use of force remains a topic of intense debate that requires further research for criminal justice practitioners and scholars. Police officers are one of the most visible arms of government, and they are entrusted with substantial authority and discretion (Bittner, 1970; Fyfe, 1988). They are the only members of society legally authorized to take life or inflict serious injury to preserve order and enforce the law (Bittner, 1970; Reiss, 1971). The public's perception of law enforcement's ability to control crime while maintaining high levels of accountably and ethical standards is often framed around the use of force by police (Adams et al., 1999; GAO, 2005, Lersch and Mieczkowski, 2005; Terrill, 2005).

During the past few decades, several incidents of excessive use of police force have garnered local, national, and international media attention (Ready, White and Fisher, 2008). These incidents have cast police in a negative light and have altered the public's perception of their use of force. Two notable examples include the 1991 Rodney King incident in Los Angeles and the 1999 shooting death of Amadou Diallo by New York City police officers (Belotto, 2001; Meyer, 1992). Both of these incidents galvanized public opinion on when and how much force law enforcement officers should use when encountering noncompliant or potentially violent suspects.

To address the public's perception of excessive use of force by officers in non-deadly force confrontations, many police agencies have adopted a variety of less-than-lethal alternatives for officers to employ when dealing with noncompliant suspects. The implementation of these less-than-lethal weapons was designed to provide officers with options to control suspects without inflicting permanent injury. The infliction of serious injuries to suspects during encounters with police is often a catalyst for citizen complaints, lawsuits, and increased scrutiny of police actions (Smith, Petrocelli and Scheer, 2006).

One of these alternatives is the conducted energy device (CED), also referred to as an electronic control weapon (ECW), or a taser (McBride and Tedder, 2005). This type of weapon has been used by police since the 1970s, but it has recently gained renewed popularity with the development of a new generation of products. Nationally, a limited number of deaths and injuries have occurred during taser use (McBride and Tedder, 2005, p.6). While the number of deaths is small when compared to overall taser uses many of these incidents have generated intense media coverage (Amnesty International, 1999, 2004). Research has shown that often the facts in these cases have been exaggerated and misrepresented to the public (Ready, White and Fisher, 2008). These cases are a clear indication that the lack of substantive research on the use and effects of taser technology leaves many unanswered questions for both the police and the public.

Police officers are authorized to use force in very specific circumstances; these are dictated by agency policies and are sanctioned by state statutes and federal laws. Police also receive extensive training in use-of-force methods. Individual state policing standards guidelines mandate this training annually (GAO, 2005). Officers routinely encounter situations when use of force is appropriate (NIJ, 1998, p.38). Research by Adams et al. (1999) found that officers used or threatened force in only a small percentage of police-citizen encounters based on survey responses from citizens. Most of these encounters involve a limited use of force, such as detaining, handcuffing, and searching suspects, and prior to making arrests (Adams et. al., 1999; Garner and Maxwell, 1999; McLaughlin, 1992; Stetser,

2001; Terrill, 2001). Limited force may also be used with suspects who are noncompliant or combative (Croft, 1986); typical examples include restraining unruly combatants, confronting armed suspects, or controlling disruptive demonstrators (Garner, Buchanan, Schrade and Hepbern, 1996; McLaughlin, 1992). When suspects are only resisting the actions or commands of officers but not physically resisting in use of force encounters they are only offering passive level resistance. When that resistance escalates to physical movements to either resist the actions of the officer or escape, this escalation is considered active physical resistance. This distinction is one of the key elements of this study and this terminology has been used by many police agencies to describe levels of resistance when developing use-of-force guidelines and policies.

Research by Adams et al. (1999) has shown that most police use of force involves the use of weaponless tactics, such as grabbing or holding, to control suspects. Police typically use force when they are trying to make an arrest and the suspect resists. Police use weapons in about two percent of all arrests (Adams et al., 1999). The weapon most frequently used was chemical spray (1.2 percent of all arrests). Firearms were the least often used (0.2 percent) (Adams et al., 1999).

According to Adams et al. (1999), "The kinds of police actions that most arouse the public's concerns—such as fatal shootings, severe beatings with fists or batons that lead to hospitalization, and choke holds that cause unconsciousness or even death—are not the typical situations in which police use force" (p.5). Most injuries that occur as a result of the use of force are more likely to be minor such as bruises or abrasions (Adams et al., 1999; Alpert and Dunham, 1997; Lundstrom and Mullan, 1987).

Most police officers are trained to use force incrementally along a Use-of-Force Continuum (Alpert and Dunham, 1997; Conner, 1991; Garner, Schade, Hepburn, and Buchanan, 1995; McLaughlin, 1992; Terrill, 2003). Supreme Court decisions and police policies dictate that officers use the minimum amount of force necessary to accomplish their mission (*Graham vs. Connor*

(109 S.Ct.1986 [1989]). Part of this progression in force involves the incremental application of a variety of use-of-force tools and tactics designed to counter or defeat the resistance of a suspect. The number and sophistication of these tools has increased significantly over the last few decades. Historically, officers only had their hands or nightsticks to use before escalating to firearms. Modern force continuums contain several other measures or tools to employ prior to using deadly force. Many of these alternatives are new technologies developed to provide options for officers to use in specific situations. The Use-of-Force Continuum provides a guide for the incremental and proportional use of these options when encountering resistance (Bittner, 1970; Conner, 1991; Terrill, 2001, 2003; Terrill and Paoline, 2007). Table 1 provides an example of a Use-of-Force Continuum. A short history of these alternatives is then provided.

Table 1: Use-of-Force Continuum

Use-of-Force Continuum	
Suspect Resistance	*Officer Use of Force*
1. No resistance	1. Officer Presence
2. Verbal noncompliance	2. Verbal commands
3. Passive resistance	3. Hands-on tactics, Chemical spray
4. Active resistance	4. Intermediate weapons: Baton, Taser, Strikes, Non-deadly force
5. Aggressive resistance	5. Intermediate weapons-Intensified techniques, Non-deadly force
6. Deadly force resistance	6. Deadly force

Adapted from the Orlando Police Department's Resistance and Response Continuum and (Terrill, 2003)

THE APPLICATION OF TECHNOLOGY TO POLICE USE OF FORCE

Police leaders have most often looked to technology to address public concerns resulting from police/citizen confrontations that require use of force. The technologies typically sought are less-than-lethal alternatives to the more traditional means of controlling suspects, such as impact weapons or weaponless tactics (Villa and Morris, 1999). These alternatives were once only available to special weapons teams who dealt with barricaded suspects, making high-risk apprehensions, or controlling large-scale civil disturbances (Bailey, 1996). In the last few decades, however, police have systematically main-streamed these weapons into the conventional police workforce. Prior to the introduction of these less-than-lethal alternatives, officers had very limited ways of escalating from empty-handed tactics to deadly force.

Impact weapons, such as the nightstick or billy club, have been used for centuries by police (Villa and Morris, 1999). Variants of the baton or nightstick became popular with law enforcement in the 1980s and early 1990s. These include side-handled and expandable batons (Truncale, 1996). The public outcry after the Rodney King beating by Los Angeles police in 1991 focused on the baton as a brutal, barbaric, and antiquated police weapon (Meyer, 1992).

While police continue to carry and use impact weapons, the focus of police research and manufacturers of use-of-force technology has shifted to developing less-than-lethal weapons that reduce the frequency of permanent injuries and allow officers to incapacitate suspects while still maintaining a safe distance (Bleetman, 2004). These modern and sophisticated offerings, such as Oleoresin Capsicum (OC) sprays; conducted energy devices, such as tasers or stun guns; and bean bag projectiles, achieve this goal with varying degrees of success and reduced amounts of unintended or unnecessary injuries (Lumb and Friday, 1997; McBride and Tedder, 2005).

THE USE OF CHEMICAL SPRAY BY POLICE

The use of chemical sprays. by police officers began in the 1980s. These weapons immediately gained popularity as alternatives to impact weapons or empty-handed tactics to gain compliance. Chemical sprays inflict less traumatic injuries than impact weapons, and they are seen as a less violent way of addressing noncompliant or violent offenders (Kaminski, Edwards, and Johnson, 1998, 1999; Morabito and Doerner, 1997).

While generally seen as effective by the police, certain types of chemical sprays have been criticized for being linked to deaths of suspects, and they are also susceptible to inappropriate use by officers (Lumb and Friday, 1997). Research into the effectiveness of chemical sprays has validated, to some extent, their use. Several studies of OC spray use by police agencies have documented higher rates of incapacitation and a reduction of injuries to suspects (Alpert and Smith, 2000; Kaminski et al., 1998; 1999; Morabito and Doerner, 1997).

A two-year study by the Federal Bureau of Investigation (FBI) found that of the 899 subjects exposed to OC spray none of the subjects suffered ill effects or adverse reactions (Weaver, 1989). In the early 1990s, there were claims that pepper spray was implicated as a contributing factor in some in-custody deaths. OC spray can compromise breathing in some people who may suffer from asthma or other breathing ailments (Kaminski, et al, 1998). In response to those claims, the International Association of Chiefs of Police (IACP) and the National Institute of Justice (NIJ) conducted a study of the pepper spray use by police and related in-custody deaths. The study's findings were that pepper spray alone was not the cause of the deaths. The study identified that positional asphyxia, the positioning of the suspect's body during transport or detention, subsequent to the use of spray may have been a contributing factor in these cases (NIJ, 1998).

The principal criticism of chemical spray, from police officer's perspective, is from the overspray that occurs when the chemical is deployed (NIJ, 1998). Officers are exposed frequently to the chemicals from the spray while securing or transporting suspects or from inhaling the fumes that are suspended in the air after a deployment. This can potentially incapacitate them and put them at risk for being disarmed or overpowered. In addition, innocent bystanders or assisting officers also can be the unintended recipient of overspray (Adkins, 2003). The accuracy of chemical sprays is much less than that of conventional firearms (Adang and Mensink, 2004; Bowling and Gaines, 2000).

THE USE OF CONDUCTED ENERGY DEVICES BY POLICE

Conducted energy devices encompass a wide range of weapons that rely on electrical shock to incapacitate combative and/or noncompliant suspects. These include stun guns, stun belts, electronic control weapons, and tasers (Cronin and Ederheimer, 2006). These weapons are the latest developments in a succession of less-than-lethal products developed and employed by both police and the military (McEwen, 1997; Meyer, 1992).

There are primarily two types of electronic control weapons. The first type of these weapons uses two metal probes that are pressed directly into the skin or clothing of a suspect. These are designated direct contact weapons. When the probes on the front of the weapon make contact this completes a circuit that delivers an electrical shock to the suspect. This electrical charge debilitates the suspect by convulsing muscles and momentarily disrupting the central nervous system (Cronin and Ederheimer, 2006). The second type of device fires two darts with hooks connected to the weapon by thin wires, which conduct the electric charge (Nielsen, 2001). When the darts penetrate the suspect's skin or clothing, a circuit is completed and an electrical charge is delivered (Williams, 2001).

The primary benefit of these weapons is that they typically incapacitate a suspect very quickly. Direct contact stun weapons incapacitate suspects by causing pain and loss of muscle control. This control is only maintained while the weapon is in direct contact with the suspect. These weapons require the operator to remain in close contact with the suspect during the encounter. This can be potentially dangerous for the operator when the weapon is disengaged and the suspect must then be secured (Kornblum, 1991). This same problem was discussed with the use of OC spray. Officers who are in close proximity to suspects during an encounter can be exposed unintentionally to overspray (Adkins, 2003).

The incapacitating effect of the dart-firing electrical shocking device can be instantaneous, and it lasts for several seconds. This is usually sufficient time to allow the suspect to be properly restrained. The dart-firing device also can be reactivated repeatedly if more time is required for restraint or backup. "Once the flow of electrical current stops, the suspect recovers rapidly, generally from several seconds to a few minutes" (Nielson, 2001, p.61).

One of the main benefits of direct contact conducted energy devices is that they can be used in a confined space. The maximum range for these weapons is the length of the arm of the person employing it. The dart firing weapons have a maximum range of 15 to 21 feet. The barbs can be discharged at very close range, but are most effective at a minimum distance of 3 feet from the operator. These weapons rely on the same "point, aim, and shoot" technique used in traditional firearms training. They are small, portable and can be fired with only one hand (Nielson, 2001, p.59).

THE INTRODUCTION OF TASERS AS A LESS-THAN-LETHAL ALTERNATIVE FOR POLICE

TASER is an acronym for Thomas A. Swift Electric Rifle, named after Tom Swift, of the popular American Children's adventure series of the 1920s and 1930s (IACP, 2004). Taser technology has been used by law enforcement agencies since 1974 (GAO, 2005; Nielson, 2001). The device was invented by Jack Cover, a NASA scientist who had experimented with electricity as a non-deadly weapon during the 1960s. The original versions of the taser used gunpowder to fire the electronic probes and, therefore, were classified as firearms under the 1968 Gun Control Act (IACP, 2004). Cover discovered that immediate incapacitation almost always occurred with no other direct negative side effects when tasers were applied to human beings in short duration (Griffith, 2002; Nielson, 2001).

Modern tasers have been modified significantly to address design flaws and to improve reliability and effectiveness (Cronin and Ederheimer, 2006; GAO, 2005, NIJ, 2008). The latest models feature a nitrogen gas propulsion system that fires two darts from a maximum distance of 21 feet, at 200-220 feet per second. The probes impact and penetrate ¼ inch into clothing or bare skin, delivering 10-20 pulses per second of 50,000 volts of electrical shock. The recipient feels a series of "rabbit punches" or "boxer's jabs" (Vogel, 1998, p. 49). Each of these shocks ensures the target suspect is "off balance, confused, and unable to aggress while the recipient of the action" (p. 49). The electric charge, which causes an interruption of the recipient's neuromuscular messages and muscle contractions, seeks a path of least resistance to reach the companion dart (Vogel, 1998).

THE CONTROVERSY SURROUNDING TASER USE BY POLICE

The use of tasers by police is not without criticism. Since their inception as a less-than-lethal alternative for police, tasers have evoked strong reactions from those who oppose their use (Cronin and Ederheimer, 2006; McBride and Tedder, 2005). Many critics of tasers compare their use to the use of electronic cattle prods as implements of torture. Both tasers and batons were used by Los Angeles police officers during the Rodney King beating incident (Meyer, 1992). This incident and the violence that ensued from this use-of-force encounter became a focal point for criticism of the police over excessive force issues. One of the primary issues with taser use is when officers should be authorized to use them. The Use-of-Force Continuum is the mechanism that guides police use of force and establishes what level of resistance must be present before various use-of-force methods can be used (Conner, 1991). The interpretation of what is excessive in a given situation often is based on the placement of use-of-force methods on the Use-of-Force Continuum.

During the last two decades, various articles from periodicals and newspapers have detailed the criticisms of the use of tasers by public safety agencies. A 1997 report by Amnesty International titled "Recent Cases of the Use of Electroshock Weapons for Torture or Ill-Treatment" lists the United States in the same class as Algeria and China with respect to human rights violations (Amnesty International, 1997). The report alleges that the taser is misused by police during use-of-force incidents. "Amnesty International and the American Civil Liberties Union both claim that these devices are unsafe and may actually encourage sadistic acts by police officers and prison guards" (Cusac, 1997, p.29). In 2004, Amnesty International called for a moratorium on the use of these weapons until an independent inquiry on the use and effects of the taser was conducted (Amnesty International, 2004). Even police agencies' opinions on the use of tasers by their officers conflict.

A Milwaukee Police report noted that 70 percent of persons hit with tasers during a 12-week period suffered some type of injury although none was serious (Diedrich, 2004). Statistics from the Los Angeles Police Department, compiled during a three-year period, show that tasers were effective at controlling suspects only 56% of the time (Hamilton, 2002). In Orange County, Florida, the sheriff office's use of tasers resulted in a decrease of OC spray and baton use by officers; however, the total number of use-of-force incidents increased by 58 percent over three years (Berenson, 2004). Citing concerns about the safety of tasers, the Department of Homeland Security has voiced its objection to deploying these devices to 20,000 agents in their two largest law enforcement divisions, Customs Enforcement and Customs Border Protection (Wilkening, 2005).

THE MEDICAL CONTROVERSY SURROUNDING THE USE OF TASERS

The medical community also is conflicted about the potential harmful effects of taser use. A February 2002 *Time Magazine* article cited a medical review conducted at the Cleveland Clinic.

Dr. Patrick Tchou, a cardiologist, reviewed the few existing scientific studies on stun guns and concluded that there is "...some potential for harm, such as irregular heartbeat, that could lead to death" (Hamilton, 2002, p. 50). According to Amnesty International, more than 150 people have died after being shocked by tasers (Berenson, 2006). This claim is adamantly denied by Taser International, a leading manufacturer of taser products (TASER International, 2004). According to a July 19, 2004, Taser International press release, "The fact is that TASER devices have never been named as the primary cause of death in any in-custody death, and any links as a contributing factor are subjective and unsupported by clear evidence" (p.2).

Amnesty International's claim is also refuted by the United Kingdom's Defense Scientific Advisory Council's subcommittee on the medical implications of less-than-lethal weapons. That study concluded that the risk of life threatening or serious injuries from the M26 Advanced Taser appears to be very low (DOMILL, 2004). Research supports that many of the deaths associated with the use of tasers involved subjects exhibiting signs of stimulant or alcohol use when engaged in confrontations with the police. This phenomenon has been labeled "excited delirium," a condition brought on by physical exertion or stress during a physical struggle in combination with these substances in the body (Cronin and Ederheimer, 2006; Fish and Geddes, 2001; Kornblum, 1991; Marks, 2005; OCSO task force, 2005; Strote and Hutson, 2006). This finding is not unexpected as many suspects are under the influence of substances when encountered by police.

The use of tasers in combination with chemical sprays also has generated public concern. Early forms of pepper spray contained mixtures that contained flammable materials, such as isopropyl alcohol, dymel, and methylene chloride (NIJ, 1998, p.43). These mixtures created controversy during a 1991 incident involving New York City Police officers who used the taser on a barricaded subject after chemical spray failed to subdue him. The subject caught fire when hit by the taser's electric current, which ignited the flammable mixture from the spray (Jett, 1997).

PROPONENTS OF TASER USE

The popularity of the taser with law enforcement agencies is clearly on the rise. According to Taser International, the weapons are used by almost 10,000 police departments in the United States and abroad (Berenson, 2006). According to the Police Executive Research Forum (PERF) the use of stun technology by law enforcement agencies has increased significantly since 1999 (PERF, 2005). This increase can be attributed to an influx of a newer generation of taser weapons that are being aggressively marketed to police agencies (Cronin and Ederheimer, 2006). Sales figures for TASER International Inc., the principal supplier of tasers to law enforcement agencies, indicate the company's revenue has increased from around "$2.2 million in 1999, to an estimated $67 million for fiscal year 2004" (McBride and Tedder, 2005, p.8). Across the United States, police agencies are purchasing and equipping their officers with the newest taser products. Presently, about 130,000 officers in 7,000 police departments are armed with tasers and, in some cities, such as Miami and Phoenix, every police officer is equipped with a taser (Wilkening, 2005). According to the United States General Accounting Office (2005), tasers have been deployed in 70,000 actual field uses during police encounters.

Taser proponents concede that the effects of these weapons can be unpleasant but argue that the number of deaths that might be attributed to the stun gun pales in comparison to the 30,000 or so Americans who are killed each year by gunshot wounds (Cronin and Ederheimer, 2006). Taser International CEO Rick Smith states, "what our weapon does is unpleasant but it can save lives" (Hamilton, 2002, p. 50).

The primary reason for the renewed popularity of the taser is related directly to the improvements in the design and reliability of newer models (Cronin and Ederheimer, 2006). Statistics related to the ability of tasers to control resistive suspects range from "33% ineffective (Commissioner Howard Safir, NYPD) to 85% effective (per manufacturer Tasertron)" (Nielsen, 2001, p. 57). Early taser models were less powerful, operating in the 5 to 14 watt range, as opposed to more modern tasers, which generate 18 to 26 watts of power. This increased power is able to defeat or overcome even the most determined adversary (Nielsen, 2001).

The latest models are smaller and more portable, making them easier to be carried by uniformed officers. These models also contain an internal memory that can be accessed by computer to determine the time, date, and number of taser deployments during a use-of-force encounter. This memory provides police agencies a measure of control and accountability when investigating allegations of misconduct with tasers by their officers (Nielsen, 2001).

The use of tasers in Central Florida, which includes the study site the Orlando Police Department (OPD), has been the subject of considerable media coverage. The use of tasers by OPD officers as well as other area police agencies has been widely reported on by the mass media. This media coverage has fueled the public controversy over the use of tasers in low level or passive resistance confrontations. This controversy has motivated agencies to change their policies on the use of tasers in these low intensity or passive resistance encounters to restrict and mitigate taser use. These policy changes and their effect on taser usage and officer attitudes about taser use after these changes are the focus of this study.

THE BENEFITS OF THIS RESEARCH RELATED TO POLICE USE OF FORCE

This work examines an organizational policy change on the use of tasers as a less-lethal alternative for police. Since the introduction of the Use-of-Force Continuum in the late 1980's, police have used variants to guide officers' use of force (Conner, 1991). The Use-of-Force Continuum acts as a guide for the officer to incrementally and proportionally increase or decrease the type and amount of force used against noncompliant or combative suspects based on the level of resistance encountered

(Conner, 1991; Garner et al. 1996; Stetser 2001; Terrill, 2001, 2003).

The controversy over where the taser should be placed on the Use-of-Force Continuum is the impetus for the policy change. The change raised the level of resistance needed to authorize taser use. Whether suspects must be actively resisting or only passively resisting the actions of officers before tasers should be used is the critical issue among many in law enforcement circles. This study examines this issue by analyzing archival use-of-force data before and after a police department changed their policy and raised the level of force necessary to use tasers on suspects showing passive to active resistance.

The study site for this research was the Orlando Police Department (OPD) in Orlando, Florida. This agency is a mid to large sized municipal police agency located in the southeast United States. The agency employs over 700 sworn officers. OPD serves a rapidly growing and diverse population of over 217,000 residents (FDLE, 2005). In 2001, the agency adopted the taser as a less than lethal use-of-force method. The use of the taser was initially authorized in situations where suspects were offering passive resistance to officers during arrests and encounters. Almost immediately, local media reports highlighted the use of tasers on suspects who were only passively resisting officers and the deployment of tasers on children in school disturbances. Five suspects who were shot with tasers by Orange County police agencies (1 by OPD officers and 4 by Orange County Sheriff's Office [OCSO] deputies) subsequently died while in police custody (Colarossi, Leusner and Moore, 2006). This controversy led to the formation of citizen committees that reviewed taser use by both the OPD and the OCSO and made recommendations (OCSO Task Force, 2005). In June 2004, Orange County Sheriff Kevin Beary conducted a televised demonstration of taser use. He allowed himself to be shot with a taser as a demonstration of the safety of the taser as a less-than-lethal weapon. Also in June 2004, the Chief of Police in Orlando changed his agency's use of force policy, raising the authorized level for deployment of the taser from passive to active resistance. It is this change and the effect on taser deployments that are the subject of this study. These events demonstrate the climate of public and media interest in taser usage in the Central Florida area during the summer of 2004. The influence that this attention had on taser use by officers and policy decisions by police leaders cannot be understated or accurately measured.

If taser deployments fell after the change in organizational policy, it provides evidence that not only are officers using this weapon in accordance with policy but also that the placement of electronic control weapons use may actually be placed correctly in the Use-of-Force Continuum associated with active resistance. However, if there was no change in the use of tasers (controlling for situational exigencies), it may indicate that, despite the change in policy, the police culture in this jurisdiction (and possibly others) may be stronger than policy directives handed down by the administrative cadre. To conduct this analysis, the research examines archival records in the period before and after the change in policy and officers were asked directly how this policy has changed their use patterns. It is hoped that this combination of methods will allow this research to blaze a new path in research that will match police practice, culture, and administrative policy directives.

To better understand police use of tasers and to examine what constitutes its effectiveness as a less-than-lethal weapon, it is necessary to review the literature related to not just police weapons, but also to the role of police and the issue of police use of force. This examination will provide a short summary of the evolving police mission and the role of technology in how police deal with the issue of use of force.

CHAPTER TWO:

A Brief History of Police Use of Force and Summary of Current Research

The evolution of policing in America has exposed a myriad of problems and challenges for police leaders and criminal justice practitioners (Vila and Morris, 1999). The vast majority of these problems and challenges have been created by the constantly evolving nature of the police mission, the increasing demands placed on police, and the sometimes unrealistic expectations of the public (Wadman and Allison, 2004). An examination of the historical progression of policing reveals a litany of problems and public scrutiny involving policing tactics (Kelling and Wycoff, 2001). Many of these problems were exacerbated by the lack of professionalism of police leaders and their cultural and institutional resistance to change (Bayley and Mendelsohn, 1969; Vila and Morris, 1999). One of the fundamental issues confronting police administrators is directing, controlling, and monitoring the use of force by their officers (Bittner, 1970; Fyfe, 1988). This issue has occupied the public's interest and has contributed to a climate of distrust and animosity between the police and the public they serve (Belotto, 2001). Many of these incidents involve the use of deadly force to apprehend or control offenders (Bayley and Garofalo, 1989). As advancements in technology created more less-than-lethal (LTL) options for officers in use-of-force confrontations, police administrators quickly grasped at them as a potential solution for these issues

(Bleetman, 2004). These options afforded officers a wider variety of methods to control suspects without having to resort to more controversial, violent, or deadly forms of force (NIJ, 1998, 2008). Often, these LTL options lacked the practical research or rigorous evaluation to support their deployment. In some incidences, this led to unintended harm to suspects or abuses by officers that have been highlighted by the mass media (Belotto, 2001; Amnesty International, 1999, 2004). This negative publicity has led to calls from the public for reform and reevaluation of these methods (Adams and Jennison, 2007).

The latest offering in LTL alternatives for police is the taser. Although the police have been using the taser since the 1970s, the newest models are more powerful and effective at rendering uncontrollable suspects compliant while minimizing officer and suspect injuries (Bozeman, Winslow, Hauda, Heck, Graham, Martin and Winslow, 2009; NIJ, 1998; GAO, 2005). Since the mid 1990s, police agencies have been issuing tasers to officers at a record pace (GAO, 2005).

What is less prevalent in the empirical research is if public perception and civil litigation led to the policy changes that attempt to alter when officers are authorized to use electronic control devices (Adams and Jennison, 2007; Smith, Petrocelli and Scheer, 2006). Additionally, more research is needed to determine if introducing these policy changes have had any substantial effect on the frequency of taser use, officer and suspect injuries, or the levels of resistance offered by noncompliant suspects.

POLICE USE OF FORCE

To fulfill their crime fighting and order maintenance roles, police must use force to restore order, take charge, or capture and control noncompliant suspects (Bittner, 1970, 1990). Incidents of force have frequently sparked criticism and controversy (Kelling and Wycoff, 2001). In an effort to improve their public image and mitigate their exposure to civil liability, police agencies have frequently sought out technology as a solution (NIJ, 1998).

In the late 1980s, Supreme Court rulings spurred changes in police procedure, prohibiting the use of deadly force simply to stop fleeing suspects. In a 1985 decision, *Tennessee v. Garner* (471 1 US [1985]), the Supreme Court held that, under the Fourth Amendment, when a law enforcement officer is pursuing a fleeing suspect, deadly force may only be used to prevent escape and only when the officer has probable cause to believe that the suspect poses a significant threat of death or serious physical injury to the officer or others (*Tennessee v. Garner*, 1985). In 1989, the Supreme Court ruled in *Graham v. Connor* (109 S.Ct.1986 [1989]) that an officer's decision regarding the level of force to use must be judged from the perspective of the reasonable person and be based on the circumstances, which are often rapidly evolving and unclear.

These landmark rulings set the standards for the Use-of-Force Continuum and for how and when police should apply force. The court recognized that officers must be able to escalate, or deescalate, levels of force to match the level of resistance presented by suspects in police/citizen encounters based on the standard of "objective reasonableness." While these rulings were instructive for police, they also forced police to explore new ways to capture or control suspects in these types of situations (Pliant, 1993). The standard of objective reasonableness is a generalized standard and is not universally understood or interpreted. This ambiguity has forced police agencies to adopt LTL policies to guide officers in use of force encounters that more clearly define and articulate what is reasonable force in a given set of circumstances.

To meet these legally imposed mandates, police agencies have relied strongly on technology to expand their options when dealing with uncooperative or noncompliant suspects. This point is made clear by the inclusion of many of these new control devices in a given agency's Use-of-Force Continuum. The goal of the continuum, and the placement of these tactics within it, is to reduce the amount of force used by officers and to lower the risk of unintentional or serious injuries to suspects or officers. Despite the recent focus on technology to control the amount of force used in specific situations, technology has a long history of shaping the practices of the police. Despite an evolution in the responsibilities placed on the police, the essential role of protecting the public has not changed that much since they were first founded in this country. The police are charged with the maintenance of order and enforcing laws. They are also seen as one of the most visible and powerful arms of government (Bittner, 1990). The use of force to advance the aims of government has always been controversial and subjective. A brief discussion of this topic is presented to provide substantive background to this issue and to clarify its relevance to this study.

THE ROLE OF POLICE IN MODERN SOCIETY

Throughout their history, police have been forced to continually reassess their role, develop new ways to fulfill their mission, and adapt in an ever-changing social and political environment. Today, police are faced with a continually expanding role in domestic security in a post 9/11 world (Wadman and Allison, 2004).

Historically, the solutions most often sought by police to meet the changing demands of the public have been grounded in new technologies to advance the delivery of police services. Despite the many technological advancements made for and by police, use of force remains a topic of debate and controversy. Often, the public's perception of the ability of police to maintain order and control crime is framed by these limited and random occurrences (Adams, et al., 1999).

In a study of the functions of police, noted criminal justice scholar Egon Bittner proposed that "the police are nothing else than a mechanism for the distribution of situationally justified force in society "(1970, p. 39). Bittner states that most police work involves stopping "something-that-ought-not-to-be-happening-and-about-which-somebody-had-better-do-something-now" (Bittner, 1970; p. 39). This statement identifies the core of the debate on how much force police should use to bring order to chaos. Bittner (1970) recognized that excessive, unnecessary, or minimal use of force by police is very difficult to define or quantify. In an attempt to provide some standards or guidance on when officers should use force, Bittner (1990) posited that because criminal law is vague, police administrators have developed taxonomies of force to guide their officer's conduct. Often, these taxonomies are manifested by "use-of-force continua," which provide a guide for officers on the types and amount of force that can be used in a given situation (Klinger, 1995).

In addressing the debate over why injuries to suspects are a natural byproduct of the police function, Bittner (1990) characterizes police as "the fire it takes to fight fire and that they in the natural course of their duties inflict harm, albeit deserved" (p.96). Unfortunately, the nature of police work is that harm is sometimes inflicted, despite the best efforts of police to control events and behavior. Police are most often called upon to interdict or stop some act of violence, unwanted behavior, or threat to public safety. This preemptive action is almost always spontaneous and not necessarily conceived by the officer. The outcome of this action is often reviewed extensively by others, both internally by police managers and by the public, typically filtered by media reports. These reviews have often raised questions and concerns about when and how much force was used to quell a disturbance or take a suspect into custody. The difference in perceptions of the public and police as to what exactly constitutes justified force contributes significantly to this debate. According to Bittner (1990):

> Though it is expected that policemen will be judicious and that experience and skill will guide them in the performance of their work, it is foolish to expect that they could always be swift and subtle. Nor is it reasonable to demand that they prevail, where they are supposed to prevail while hoping that they will always handle resistance gently (p. 97).

For some members of the public, politicians and some police administrators, the simple solution is to use less force. Fyfe (1987) discusses the negative consequences of both unnecessary force by officers and the consequences of insufficient use of force by police. The use of unnecessary force by police can lead to significant negative consequences, to include unnecessary injuries to the suspect or death, community complaints, distrust of the police, civil liability, civil unrest, and federal injunctive orders. Insufficient use of force exposes officers to harm or death, negatively affects an officer's ability to enforce the law, and increases the danger to public safety. Fyfe (1987) concludes that unnecessary force "could be avoided by measures such as better training, officer selection, and other use-of-force options" (p.6).

Much of the research and policy emphasis by police has focused on reduction of harm to officers and suspects in use-of-force confrontations. This objective forms the basis of the development of use-of-force alternatives. Use of force by police is an integral part of police work. It remains a point of controversy and debate for police practitioners and criminal justice scholars. A brief summary of this research is provided.

THE RESEARCH ON POLICE USE OF FORCE

Police are one of the few institutions of government authorized to use force (Bittner, 1970; Fyfe, 1988). The use of force by police to compel conformance to law is at the very core of their mission and purpose (Bittner, 1970). Through the use of various methods, such as field observations (Bayley and Garofalo, 1989; Friedrich, 1980; Fyfe, 1988; Terrill, 2001), conducting surveys of officers (Garner et al., 1995; Lundstrom and Millan, 1987), and examining agency use-of-force data (Alpert and Dunham, 1997, 1999; Kavanagh, 1994; Meyer, 1992; Morabito and Doerner, 1997), researchers have attempted to determine the extent to which police use and misuse force (Ederheimer and Fridell, 2005).

Various studies have also attempted to identify situational, individual and community level factors to explain why officers use force (Bayley and Garofalo, 1989; Friedrich, 1980; Riksheim and Chermak, 1993; Worden, 1995; Terrill and Mastrofski, 2002; Terrill, 2003). There is also a considerable body of research examining the area of deadly force; specifically, police use of deadly force by firearms (Binder and Fridell, 1984; Fyfe, 1979; 1980; 1988; Geller and Scott, 1992).

Generally, research on non-deadly police use of force is grouped into two distinct areas. These include studies on authorized police use of force (Bayley and Garofalo, 1989; Friedrich, 1980; Fyfe, 1988) and studies on unauthorized use of force by police (Bayley and Mendelsohn, 1969; Fyfe, 1980; Geller and Toch, 1995). Research on non-lethal force suffers from the same shortcomings as the research on lethal force; namely, an inability to define adequately what constitutes reasonable or excessive force (Bittner, 1970: 1990; Garner et al., 1995) (See Table 2).

STUDIES EXAMINING THE FACTORS THAT INFLUENCE USE OF FORCE

Friedrich (1980), using Reiss' (1969) observational data, examined what factors most significantly influence police use of force. He determined that the traditional factors that had been previously regarded as having an effect on police use of force (such as situational and organizational factors) were, in fact, not significant. Friedrich determined that situational characteristics of encounters, such as race, gender, social class, and suspect demeanor, were more predictive of police use of force.

Garner, Buchanan, Schrade, and Hepbern (1995) examined 1,585 officer surveys of use of force and conducted 185 interviews of suspects involved in use-of-force incidents. The surveys captured specific situational characteristics relevant to the officers' use of force. The suspects in these incidents were interviewed to provide insight into the dynamics of how the force was used. The study's findings supported the notion that police use force very infrequently when compared to the number of arrests made. The study found that 1 in 5 arrests required

Table 2: Studies of Police Use of Force

Author(s)	Nature of Sample	Data Date	Data Type
Fredrich (1980)	1,565 police citizen encounters in DC, Boston, and Chicago. (Reexamination of Reiss, 1969)	1966	Observational data
Croft (1985)	2,397 uses of force from 123,500 arrests made by Rochester, NY police	1973-1979	Use of force forms
Fyfe (1989)	2,142 violent encounters in Dade County FL.	1985 to 1986	Observational data
Lundstrom and Mullan (1987)	11,989 custody situations in St. Paul, Minn.	March 1985 - February 1986	Officers' use-of-force forms
Bayley and Garafalo (1989)	467 police citizen encounters in NYC	Summer 1986	Observational data
Meyer (1992)	568 use-of-force incidents involving LAPD officers	1989	Use of force forms
McLaughlin (1992)	11,000 arrests by Savannah GA. Police	1989	Use of force forms
Pate and Fridell (1993)	1,111 law enforce-ment agencies were surveyed on the use of all types of weapons and citizens' complaints	1991	Agency surveys
Kavanagh (1997)	1,108 arrests made at the NY port authority bus terminal	1990-1991	Arrest Reports
Garner et al. (1995)	1585 arrests in Phoenix, AZ.	1994	Use of force forms

Table 2, cont.

Author(s)	Nature of Sample	Data Date	Data Type
Worden (1995)	5,688 police citizen encounters in St. Louis, Missouri; Rochester, NY; and Tampa, FL	1977	Observational data
Alpert and Dunham (1997)	676 Use of force incidents in Miami-Dade County, FL	1997-1998	Use of force forms
Lumb and Friday (1997)	61 Use of force incidents in Concord, NC	July1992-December 1993	Use of force forms
Morabito and Doerner (1997)	999 Use-of- force encounters in Tallahassee, FL	1993-1995	Use of force forms
Kaminski et al. (1999)	878 OC Spray incidents in Baltimore County, MD	1993-1996	Survey data
Terrill (2001)	3,544 police encounters with suspects in St. Petersburg, FL and Indianapolis, IN	St. Petersburg, FL (Summer 1997) and Indianapolis, IN (Summer 1996)	Observational data
Terrill and Mastrofski (2002)	3,544 police encounters with suspects in St. Petersburg, FL and Indianapolis, IN	St. Petersburg, FL (Summer) 1997 and Indianapolis, IN (Summer 1996)	Observational data

police to use some physical force. Suspects offered resistance in 1 of every 6 arrests. Police use weapons in 2 percent of all arrests. A blunt force impact weapon was the weapon most frequently used (12 times in 1,585 arrests). The study found that the single best predictor of police use of force was suspect use of force (Garner et al., 1996).

Kavanagh (1997) studied arrest records from resisting arrest incidents during 1990 and 1991 at the New York Port Authority Bus Terminal. This study identified that the arrestee's behavior prior to resisting the officer's attempts to arrest was most closely associated with the officer's need to use force. These behaviors included disrespect of the officer, alcohol intoxication, and the seriousness of the original crime charged. The significance of this research is that it supports the finding that officers play a much smaller role in the occurrence of resisting arrest than previously thought.

Terrill (2001), using observational data from 3,544 police citizen encounters during the summers of 1996 and 1997 in St. Petersburg, Florida and Indianapolis, Indiana, developed the idea of using force factor scores. These scores assess not only the highest level of suspect resistance and use of force within an incident but also include all instances of resistance and force that take place. This study found that encounters that began with some form of force resulted in a greater frequency of subsequent suspect resistance and an increased use of additional force at some later point in the encounters. This study underscores the importance of understanding police use of force relative to suspect resistance (Terrill, 2005).

Terrill and Mastrofski (2002), analyzing the same observational data from police citizen encounters in St, Petersburg and Indianapolis, concluded that police used more force against non-white, younger, poorer, or intoxicated suspects who resisted police authority. Police use of force was statistically unrelated to angry, disrespectful, or mentally impaired suspects.

THE PREVALENCE OF FORCE IN POLICE CITIZEN ENCOUNTERS

The public's confidence level of police agencies can be greatly altered by a single incident of police use-of-force abuse. For this reason, police have sought to regulate use of force by officers by providing policies and guidelines that outline a steady progression of the levels of force that must be applied to gain compliance. Frequently, these levels are based on various weapons and methods authorized to respond to a corresponding level of resistance by suspects. Examinations of police use-of-force reports, excessive use-of-force complaints, and citizen or officer surveys all affirm the low incidence of police use of force in encounters with citizens (Adams, et al., 1999; Garner and Maxwell, 1999). However, each of these research methodologies has their specific strengths and weaknesses (Pate and Fridell, 1993). Observational studies have sometimes been criticized for not generating sufficient data (Garner et. al, 1995). However, more recent work by Terrill buffers this criticism (Terrill and Mastrofski, 2002; Terrill, 2003). Data on excessive force complaints can only provide indirect measures of actual behavior. Surveys and interviews tend to measure perceptions of force or excessive force, which may differ from actual events (Garner, Maxwell and Heraux, 2002). Scenario-based surveys typically do not capture accurate responses of what officers would really do in specific situations (Alpert and Smith, 1999). Agency-generated use-of-force data is often biased towards a best-case depiction of events, or it presents an agency-biased perspective (Garner et. al, 1995).

The question of how infrequently police use force has generated considerable debate among professionals. In an observational study of the frequency of the use of non-lethal force by New York police officers, Bayley and Garafalo (1989) found that officers used physical force with citizens in only 8 percent of the 467 documented encounters. This study supports other research findings in that the use of force is rare in police-citizen encounters, although their study did not distinguish between what is reasonable and unreasonable force.

Croft (1985) examined forms relating to the use of force that were completed by Rochester, New York, officers during a six-year period. This research indicated that physical force was only used against citizens in 2,397 of the 123,500 arrests made during the examination period. This reinforced the notion that police use force rarely in encounters with the public. Surprisingly, she found that the vast majority (80%) of the use-of-force incidents examined involved misdemeanors, violations, or no criminal situations.

Fyfe (1989) used observational data from a study of 2,412 potentially violent situations in Dade County, Florida. This study found that officers used force greater than a firm voice command in only 12 percent of use-of-force incidents. The greatest limitation of this study rests in its reliance on trained observers to make judgments about the levels of force used, making synthesis of the data difficult.

McLaughlin (1992), relying on official use-of-force reports of arrests in Savannah, Georgia completed during 1989, discovered only 133 use-of-force incidents in over 11,000 arrests. Of the 133 incidents, 45 involved instances in which officers punched or kicked citizens, 11 in which officers struck citizens with a baton, and 2 in which officers sprayed citizens with mace. The results of this study concluded that police used force in as low as 1 percent of the cases examined.

Adams et al. (1999) using data from the 1996 pilot test of the PPCS (Police-Public Contact Survey) found that only about 1 percent of people reporting contacts with police said that officers used or threatened force. This research found that police used physical force in less than 20 percent of 7,512 arrests studied. Weaponless tactics such as grabbing or holding were primarily used. Grabbing was the tactic used about one-half of the time. Police used weapons in only 2 percent of all arrests. When weapons were used, chemical sprays were the weapon of choice (1.2 percent of all arrests) with firearms least often used (0.2 percent).

Worden (1995), using observational data from a police services study in 60 neighborhoods surrounding St. Louis,

Missouri; Rochester, New York; and Tampa, Florida, reported that police used force in just over 1 percent of the nearly 5,700 police-citizen encounters observed. Further supporting the premise of low incidence of police use of force, Langen et al, (2001) cited findings from a 1999 Bureau of Justice Statistics national survey, which reported that 1 percent of the people reporting face-to-face contact with the police experienced either force or the threat of force. However, most of the force was either threatened or at a low level.

Terrill (2003) using data collected as part of an observational study of the police in Indianapolis, Indiana, and St. Petersburg, Florida, examined 3,544 police-suspect encounters in an attempt to better understand the application of non-lethal force and the relationship between officer use of force and suspect resistance. Terrill found that multiple uses of force and resistance within individual encounters increases the frequency of both behaviors. Most suspects display forceful and resistant behaviors, which are typically on the lower end of continuum. When officers use greater levels of force early on, or any time, during an encounter the level of suspect resistance is also higher. This finding calls into question the utility of a "take charge" approach to maintaining control within police-suspect encounters.

INJURIES TO SUSPECTS IN POLICE USE-OF-FORCE ENCOUNTERS

Further research reveals that injuries to suspects from police actions occur very rarely and are often minor (Adams et al., 1999; Alpert and Dunham, 1997; Bozeman et al, 2009; Lundstrom and Mullan, 1987). Most studies on police use-of-force methods have examined injuries to suspects as a central component of their research (Alpert and Dunham 1998; Kaminski et al., 1999; Lumb and Friday, 1997; Meyer, 1991; Morabito and Doerner, 1997). Much of the research on less-than-lethal weapons relates directly to the ability of these weapons to render uncooperative or combative suspects compliant without inflicting unnecessary injury or deaths (Bozeman et al. 2009;

Strote and Hutson, 2006; White and Ready, 2007; Williams, 2008).

INJURIES TO OFFICERS IN USE-OF FORCE ENCOUNTERS

The reduction of officer injuries is one of the primary goals of policies governing use of force and it also is responsible for the advent of alternatives to traditional use-of-force methods. The effect on officer injuries from the use of LTL alternatives has been the subject of considerable research on LTL weapons (Alpert and Dunham 1998; Kaminski et al 1999; Lumb and Friday, 1997; Meyer, 1991; Morabito and Doerner, 1997) and police use of force in general (Garner et al. 1996; Garner and Maxwell, 1999; Terrill et al, 2003). Most of the research related to various use-of-force methods, such as chemical sprays (Kaminski et al, 1998), tasers (McManus et al. 2004; Hougland et al., 2005), or multiple use-of-force methods (McLaughlin, 1992; Meyer, 1992) examine changes in the frequency of injuries to officers as a measure of effectiveness.

THE POLICE USE-OF-FORCE CONTINUUM

Research also supports that officers are trained to use force progressively along a continuum (Alpert and Dunham, 1997; McLaughlin, 1992; Sykes and Brent, 1980; Terrill, 2001, 2003; Terrill, Alpert, Dunham, and Smith, 2003). Supreme Court rulings, criminal statues, and police agencies' use-of-force policies require that officers use only that level of force reasonably necessary to control or apprehend a suspect (Alpert and Dunham, 1997; Garner et al. 1996; Garner, Maxwell and Heraux, 2002; *Graham v. Conner,* 1989).

The escalation of police use of force is guided by a continuum based on a variety of methods and tools for officers to employ when resistance to their lawful authority is encountered (McLaughlin, 1992; Terrill, 2003; Terrill, Alpert, Dunham, and Smith, 2003). Terrill et al. (2003) identifies the Use-of-Force Continuum and the use-of-force reports as two of the "building blocks to gauge and assess use-of-force incidents" (p.151). When these two mechanisms are used in combination, they can greatly improve the assessment of appropriate and inappropriate levels of force. According to Terrill et al. (2003), the Use-of-Force Continuum is simply a way to characterize and examine how officers apply force in relation to the resistance they encounter. The primary objective of using the force continuum as a measure of police force is to determine the extent to which officers follow or deviate from the continuum's structure. The primary focus of the Use-of-Force Continuum is the notion of control. If the structure of the continuum is followed, the intended purpose of control has been achieved. If the continuum structure has not been followed, the use of force was deemed to be for some other unauthorized purpose (Terrill, 2005).

The Use-of-Force Continuum typically initiates with verbal commands and presence by the officer. As increasing levels of resistance to the officer's commands and attempts to control a suspect are encountered, the level of force is increased incrementally. If resistance is encountered, the level of force is increased by the use of weapons such as batons, chemical sprays, or tasers, but it can also be techniques such as empty-handed strikes or leg kicks and, ultimately, it can culminate with officers using deadly force.

Despite the infrequency of police use of force and the limited number of injuries incurred during that use of force, police brutality and excessive use of force remains at the forefront of public scrutiny and media attention (Smith, Petrocelli, and Scheer, 2006). Using this as a framework, any understanding of the public's perception of police use of force must be measured by these limited incidents.

Research on use of force has found that a variety of variables influence police use of force. These include both situational variables, such as the presence of citizen bystanders, suspect characteristics and demeanor, as well as individual level variables, such as officer characteristics. A short summary of these studies is provided.

THE RESEARCH ON VARIABLES THAT INFLUENCE POLICE USE OF FORCE

The Influence of Suspect Characteristics in Use-of-Force Encounters

A great deal of research has focused on the influence of suspect characteristics on police use of force (Friedrich, 1980; Sherman, 1980; Terrill and Mastrofski, 2002). In the area of deadly force research, the effect of race of suspects involved in police shootings has dominated the literature (Binder and Fridell, 1984; Fyfe, 1979; 1980; 1988; Geller and Scott, 1992). Research has found that black suspects are more likely to be stopped and interrogated by officers, but minority suspects are also more likely to be uncooperative with police (Black, 1971; Ferdinand and Luchterhand, 1970; Terrill et al., 2003). Suspect age and gender also has been examined as a situational variable in police use-of-force studies (Friedrich, 1980; Sherman, 1980). Research indicates that police typically perceive women to be less aggressive than men in use-of-force encounters (Croft, 1985; Klinger, 1995). There has been considerable controversy about and public scrutiny of the use of tasers on juveniles and women. Youthful offenders have been identified in the research as being perceived by police as more threatening to them than adult suspects (Faulkner, 1991; Terrill and Mastrofski, 2002). Because gender and age are areas of concern, they will be included as situational variables for analysis.

The Number of Other Officers Present During Use-of-Force Encounters

The number of officers present at the scene of an incident has been shown to influence officer's propensity to use force (Terrill and Mastrofski, 2002). The nature of the relationship of this variable to the use of force is mixed. Research has found that single officers tend to be more cautious and less prone to assert themselves in situations where force may be applied (Banton, 1964; Wilson, 1963). In general, officers have been found to act differently and are unwilling to engage in high-risk behavior when no peer support is present (Friedrich, 1977). This finding is counter intuitive to the conventional wisdom that more officers, either in a patrol car (1 officer patrol car versus 2 officers assigned to a patrol car), or on the scene of as use of force encounter, provide a measure of safety for officers. The effect of the number of officers present in use-of-force encounters is an important situational variable and, as such, will be incorporated in this study design.

The Presence of Citizen Bystanders during Police Use-of-Force Encounters

Early studies indicated that excessive force is less likely to occur in public places (Sherman, 1980; Smith, 1986). Other research has failed to link the visibility of the situation to changes in the frequency or severity of police use of force (Friedrich, 1980). The location where use of force occurs has also been a subject of prior research (Friedrich, 1980; Sherman, 1980; Smith, 1986). Additionally, studies have shown that the presence of bystanders was negatively related to the perceived necessity of drawing a weapon (Holzworth and Pipping, 1985).

THE TYPES OF INCIDENTS THAT LEAD TO USE OF FORCE

The threat or seriousness of the incident and type of incident has been found to be significant in the use of force by police officers (Bayley and Garofolo, 1989; Garner et al, 2002; Terrill, 2003). Other research has failed to conclusively relate the nature of the encounter to the levels of physical force used (Friedrich, 1980; Fyfe, 1982). Research has found that it is difficult to link definitively the nature of the incident to the resulting use of force. Some incidents begin as routine encounters or calls for police service that escalate to a use of force by the officer. Other more serious offences, with suspect apprehensions, may not result in any use of force.

Research has examined the effect of whether or not an encounter was officer initiated or a call for police service (Friedrich, 1980). Much of the criticism on the use of taser is focused on the types of encounters that lead to its use and the role of the officer in those encounters (GAO, 2005). The change in placement of the taser in the Use-of-Force Continuum was designed to reduce the use of tasers in lower-level encounters, where suspects may only be exhibiting passive resistance. Often, these types of encounters result from self-initiated, consensual police-citizen encounters, such as traffic stops, or consensual encounters with suspects in high drug sales areas (McBride and Tedder, 2005).

A variety of tools and weapons have been developed and implemented to aid police in protecting themselves and in maintaining public order. A short summary of the history of these tools is practical in any discussion of police use-of-force issues and, therefore, is presented below.

TRADITIONAL POLICE TOOLS USED TO KEEP THE PEACE

Historically, police have sought suitable tools to control the behavior of criminals. Impact weapons were one of the first weapons sued by police. The "billy club," also known as a "truncheon" was issued to London's Bobbies in the late 1820s (Truncale, 1996). British police leaders sought a weapon that was not immediately intimidating to citizens. The truncheon was small enough to be concealed in the pocket of a coat or in trousers, but, when needed, it was effective for rendering an unruly suspect compliant (Truncale, 1996).

Nightsticks, Flashlights, and Batons

Officers have been provided with a variety of impact weapons since the inception of organized policing (Peak, 1990). The first police nightsticks or batons used by American police were made of wood and were standard issue for most police departments well into the 1980s. The next generation of baton was developed in 1958 by William Bailey and was known as a monadnock™ or PR-24 baton. It had a side handle, which was mounted at a 90-degree angle. This weapon was very effective and was adopted for use by police agencies throughout the 1970s and 1980s. It afforded officers a wider range of defensive techniques and an increased capability to defeat an adversary in a hand-to-hand confrontation (Truncale, 1996).

The problem of portability for officers who must carry an array of equipment created the need for the expandable baton (Ederheimer and Fridell, 2005). Expandable batons have only been used by police since the 1980's; they consist of metal tubes that lock into place with a snap of the wrist. The disadvantage of expandable batons is that they may collapse with a hard strike to an immovable surface. Expandable batons lack the durability of a traditional fixed baton. The latest styles of expandable batons are made from a combination of polycarbonate and metal and automatically lock in place to prevent collapse (NIJ, 1998).

Flashlights have also been a standard issue with police since their inception. The flashlight as a weapon of choice has at times been a topic of police research. Several incidents of unnecessary force or even death have been attributed to police use of the flashlight as an impact weapon. This use as a blunt force impact weapon remains controversial (Cox, Faughn and Nixon, 1985).

Firearms as a Law Enforcement Tool

Despite the fact that firearms were essential in the creation of the government of the United States after breaking away from British rule, the use of firearms by police was not immediately accepted by the citizenry of the newly formed United States (Villa and Morris, 1999). The fear of a standing army and centralized authority had not abated since the revolution, and, for many people, the police represented both. The uncertain role of police and the influence of local politics made armed police an unpopular choice for most cities (Wadman and Allison, 2004). Even though firearms were used regularly by criminals, and possessed by even ordinary citizens, uniformed officers and watchman were not authorized to carry firearms in most major U.S. cities until the middle part of the 19th century (Wadman and Allison, 2004). After the killings of several officers by gun wielding criminals, the police in most metropolitan cities were issued revolvers for self-protection (Bailey, 1995). New York City police officers were issued Colt .32 caliber revolvers in the 1890s, and other east coast cities, such as Philadelphia and Boston, quickly followed suit (Bailey, 1995). Some police departments, such as the Phoenix Police Department, did not arm their police until 1911 (NIJ, 1998). It was not until the 1920 and 1930s that the arming of police gained widespread acceptance in America. The .32 caliber Colt revolver remained the weapon of choice for most agencies well into the 20th century (Wadman and Allison, 2004).

As the frequency of police shootings increased during the 1960s and 1970s, many agencies upgraded their weapons to more powerful revolvers (Bailey, 1996; NIJ, 1998). It was not until the 1980s that police agencies began to transition from revolvers to semi-automatic pistols for officers. This transition was in response to a wave of violent crime in most large American cities during the 1980s, which left police feeling outgunned by their criminal counterparts (Geller and Scott, 1992).

Several highly publicized and controversial fatal police shootings during this time period sparked widespread civil unrest in several major U.S. cities (Kelling and Wycoff, 2001). These controversies motivated police agencies to seek alternatives to deadly force for their officers. These alternatives were manifested in the form of a wide range of tools and weapons designed to incapacitate offenders, without inflicting unnecessary harm or death. Prior to this time period, these weapons had been the exclusive purview of the military or the special weapons units within most major police departments. The mainstreaming of these weapons to conventional police forces was a significant change for most agencies. These options became known as less-than-lethal weapons (LTL).

LESS-THAN-LETHAL WEAPONS FOR POLICE

There is substantial peer-reviewed research on the subject of non-lethal alternatives for police (Geller and Scott, 1992; Homant and Kennedy, 2000; Lumb and Friday, 1997; McEwen and Leahy, 1993; McEwen, 1997; Meyer, 1992; Morabito and Doerner, 1997; Parent, 2000; Peak, 1990). The term "non-lethal" weapon is often misunderstood or misinterpreted as being euphemistic or an oxymoron. Most non-lethal technologies have inflicted lethal results if improperly employed or under very unique circumstances (Lewer, 2003). For this reason, the term "less-than-lethal" has been more readily accepted. Any use of force that is not designed to kill could be defined as less-than-lethal. The traditional definition for less-than-lethal weapons are those designed to render a suspect compliant using force less than is designed to be lethal (Lamb, 1995).

Lamb (1995) posits, "nonlethal weapons are discriminate weapons that are explicitly designed and employed so as to incapacitate personnel or material, while minimizing fatalities and undesired damage to property and environment. Unlike weapons that permanently destroy targets through blast, fragmentation, or penetration, nonlethal weapons have relatively reversible effects on targets and/or are able to discriminate between targets and non-targets in the weapon's area of impact" (p.1).

The concept of non-lethal weapons is also attractive to politicians. Most police agencies responding to criticism about the use of deadly force have sought more humane methods for dealing with unruly mobs, arresting violent criminals, and controlling emotionally disturbed people (Lewer, 2003).

Less-than-lethal weapons were first introduced to law enforcement in the early 1970s (Robin, 1996). The development of these weapons was motivated by historical events and initiatives at both the local and federal level. The 1967 Presidential Crime Commission report, *The Challenge of Crime in a Free Society,* identified the need for police to seek alternatives to deadly force. The 308-page report contained 200 recommendations for the development of policies and technologies to fight crime. As a result of this report and its recommendations, millions of federal dollars flowed into crime fighting initiatives and technologies (Kelling and Wycoff, 2001).

The landmark United States Supreme Court decision, *Tennessee v. Garner* (1985), which prohibited police from using deadly force to apprehend unarmed or nonviolent fleeing felony suspects, also fueled the development of alternatives to deadly force (Pilant, 1993). A subsequent National Institute of Justice (NIJ) report also called for the development of alternatives for police in lieu of deadly force (NIJ, 1998). This spurred great interest in funding research for a wide range of less-than-lethal alternatives for law enforcement officers. The Rodney King incident in Los Angeles galvanized public opinion regarding excessive use of force by police and spurred the creation of an independent city commission on use-of-force issues. The commission also made recommendations that called for more alternatives for police to deal with nonviolent but noncompliant offenders (Meyer, 1992). Various authors have cited the need for continued expansion and exploration of less-than-lethal alternatives for police (Bailey, 1996; Garner et al., 1996; Homant and Kennedy, 2000; Lumb and Friday, 1997; McEwen, 1993; McEwen, 1997; Meyer, 1992; Morabito and Doerner, 1997; Parent, 2000; Peak, 1990).

An analysis of policy development can provide insight into how policy on less-than-lethal (LTL) force has driven the development of LTL weapons and tactics. McEwen (1997) reviewed the use-of-force policies from 96 law enforcement agencies. The study concluded that LTL weapons policies influenced the levels of police shootings. The two significant findings of this study were an increasing reliance on OC spray by officers in many police departments and the identification of a significant number of agencies with inconsistent policies that define lethal and non-lethal force. The significance of this study to the current area of investigation is that simply providing officers with this type of weaponry and training is insufficient (McEwen, 1997).

The effect of LTL weapons on the killing of citizens by police was the subject of a 1996 study. Bailey (1996) used national data for large U.S. cities for the year 1990 to examine the relationship between the availability of various types of LTL weapons and the rates of police-citizen killings for the public, in general, and by race, in particular. This study found no evidence that the availability of LTL weapons reduced the number of police killings of citizens. The limitations of this report are its use of FBI data on justifiable homicide rates and the limitations of the data that indicate the availability of LTL weapons by the agencies chosen (Bailey, 1996).

MODERN LESS-THAN-LETHAL WEAPONRY

A wide range of LTL options and tactics has been developed that provide alternatives for officers to employ when dealing with unruly or combative violators. These options can be deployed against individual suspects who are resisting police actions, or in situations involving multiple suspects in a riot or civil disorder. A variety of LTL projectiles, such as rubber or wooden bullets and gas munitions, have been developed for use on physically combative or barricaded suspects, or for use in disturbances with multiple suspects. Typically, these options allow the officer to deploy weapons against potentially armed or violent suspects at a safe distance. Other options, such as impact weapons, chemical sprays, or electronic control devices, are designed for use by a lone officer against single or multiple combative offenders in close proximity. Each of these use-of-force options has strengths and limitations. A short summary of the history of these weapons and a summary of the evaluative research of their use are presented for illustration.

Chemical Sprays

One LTL alternative that gained popularity with police is the use of chemical sprays. A variety of chemical sprays have been developed and used by both the military and the police since the mid-1960s. These include CN, CS, and OC spray. CN gas (Chloroacetaphenone), or tear gas, was introduced for police use in the 1960s. Its principle use was in civil disorders or riots. It is an irritant that produces burning in the eyes, nose, and throat. CS gas (Ortho/Chlorobenzal-Malononitrile), .another disabling gas, also came into use during the 1960s and 1970s. CS gas causes pain in the nose, throat, and chest. It also can cause nausea and vomiting, and it is considered more potent than CN gas (Alpert and Smith, 2000).

The latest chemical spray to be developed and used by police is Oleoresin Capsicum (OC) spray. The original versions of this spray developed in the 1980s were known as "mace" and were initially used by the U.S Postal Service Carriers (Geller and Scott, 1992, p. 378). OC spray is derived from an irritant in cayenne pepper and is one of the more popular and effective products on the market today (Alpert and Smith, 2000; Meyer, 1992). The police have used it extensively since its inception as a LTL weapon.

McEwen and Leahy (1993) estimate that 41% of the major public safety agencies in the United States equip their personnel with OC spray. In a survey of 378 police and Sheriff's departments, McEwen and Leahy (1993) found that 65 percent of responding agencies issue chemical sprays to their officers. Alpert and Smith (2000) also found that OC spray is widely used by agencies with more than 100 officers. A number of studies have been conducted on the use of OC spray by police. These studies have used a variety of methods to explain and evaluate the use of OC spray.

Case Studies of OC Spray Implementation

In one of the more comprehensive studies on the use of chemical spray, Morabito and Doerner (1997) examined police use of OC spray in the Tallahassee, Florida Police Department (TPD). The study used 563 use-of-force forms completed by the officers between 1993 and 1995. The results of the study revealed that the use of OC spray results in fewer and less severe officer and offender injuries relative to impact weapons (batons and flashlights). OC spray was effective only three-quarters of the time it was deployed; however, it did neutralize a wide spectrum of suspects. The level of effectiveness of OC spray in the study sample fell far below the manufacturer's claims for the type of spray used by the TPD. Morabito and Doerner (1997) identified many of the strengths and weaknesses of the use of OC spray as a LTL weapon. The fact that OC allows the officer to remain at a distance and still exercise some control over a noncompliant suspect and the fact that injuries to officers and suspects are greatly reduced by OC use is significant. The study also identified the tendency of officers to move into close proximity with suspects who are believed to be armed or who appear to be more dangerous to them. This would tend to be a detractor for the use of OC spray. It would seem to indicate a lack of confidence in the spray by officers or an unwillingness to rely on it in these types of confrontations. The lack of effectiveness of the OC product studied might also be relevant to this line of reasoning. If the officers lacked confidence in the product, they might be less inclined to use it in more serious or hazardous situations.

Kaminski, Edwards, and Johnson (1999) studied the use of OC spray by the Baltimore County, Maryland, Police Department. The study examined 878 uses of uses of OC spray from July 1993 to December 1996. Their findings indicated officers reported an 85 percent effectiveness rate in making arrests. However, a much lower rate of effectiveness was noted with mentally disturbed or intoxicated suspects.

The implementation of OC spray by a single agency was the subject of a study by Atkins (2003). This study examined the use of OC spray by a medium-sized municipal police agency between 1999 and 2001. Using primarily self-reported data, OC deployments were examined to determine their effectiveness as a LTL technology for police. The results of the study revealed that while the frequency of injuries to officers during the examination period decreased, the number of excessive use-of-force complaints increased. The limitations of this study lie in its use of officers' self-reported data and the inability of findings to be generalized to a larger population (Adkins, 2003). This study, like many others, fails to resolve or address the central question: Would officers have resorted to this level of force if they did not have OC spray available to them? More succinctly, what effect(s) do the availability of LTL alternatives have on the levels of force used and the number of excessive use-of-force complaints filed by citizens?

A study by Bowling and Gaines (2000) examined officer and suspect injuries and excessive force complaints during the deployment of OC spray by officers in three North Carolina law enforcement agencies during a two-year period from 1997 through 1998. The agencies studied were the Winston Salem Police Department, the Charlotte-Mecklenburg Police Department, and the North Carolina State Highway Patrol. The study used self-reported use-of-force data by officers and queried suspect injury and excessive force complaint data information from agency records. The study found the use of OC spray was associated with declines in the number of injuries to NC Highway Patrol officers and complaints of excessive use of force. It also found a strong association with OC use and reduction of injuries to suspects and overall officer use of force in one of the agencies. The results of this study highlight the difficulty with generalizing any finding to the community of law enforcement. The data captured in the use-of-force forms examined did not relate the same information in a consistent way from all of the agencies. The lack of consistent use-of-force and injury data from all of the study sites contributed to the inability to link OC spray use to changes in the identified study categories (Bowling and Gaines, 2000).

Another LTL tool that has gained popularity with law enforcement is the conducted energy device, electronic control weapon, or taser. Conducted energy devices, or electronic control weapons, encompass a wide range of products and weapons that use electricity to incapacitate a suspect. Electronic control weapons include the taser and stun guns.

Tasers

Taser technology has been in service with law enforcement agencies since 1974 (IACP, 2004). A number of articles are available from publications on specific taser products (Nielson, 2001; Vogel, 1998; Williams, 2001). These articles primarily discuss product features or innovations to specific models, or they track the progression in product development. These publications do not specifically discuss or evaluate the effectiveness or characteristics of operational taser deployments. A review of current literature reveals limited research on police use of taser in conjunction with situational variables, such as suspect characteristics, the types of incidents which lead to taser use, or the number of officers or bystanders present. There are a limited number of research studies that examine taser use in conjunction with other LTL use-of-force methods. Several studies examine taser use by single agencies. A brief summary of these studies is presented.

Case Studies of the Use of Tasers

In one of the more comprehensive studies of use of force by a police agency, Meyer (1992) evaluated statistics of taser, (OC) chemical spray, and a variety of other use-of-force methods. The study examined 568 use-of-force reports from the Los Angeles Police Department (LAPD) during 1989. These incidents involved a variety of non-lethal tactics deployed on suspects. These tactics included the use of batons, flashlights, karate kicks, punches, swarming (several officers rushing the suspect), chemical sprays, and taser deployments. The injuries sustained by suspects and officers from each type of force were compared. The suspects' injuries were classified into three groups based on severity, using major, moderate, and minor categories. The over-all findings of this study were remarkable with respect to injuries inflicted by impact weapons when compared to other types of use-of-force methods (Illustrated in Table 3).

The significance of this research study is that the rates of injury to suspects and officers were shown to be significantly reduced when tasers or chemical sprays were used. The use of other force methods resulted in increased levels of both officer and suspect injuries. This study was one of the first practical studies to examine taser use in an operational context when compared to other LTL use-of-force methods. The limitations of this study could be argued as the relative low number (102 cases) of taser and chemical spray deployments.

Table 3: Officer and Suspect Injury Rates by Type of Force Used LAPD

Force Type	Study Cases	Injury to Officers	Injury to Suspects
Baton	143	23 (16%)	86 (60%)
Kick	47	5 (11%)	12 (26%)
Punch	36	13 (36%)	28 (64%)
Miscellaneous bodily force	143	21 (15%)	66 (46%)
Flashlight	25	1 (4%)	20 (80%)
Swarm	51	8 (16%)	12 (24%)
Chemical spray	21	0 (0%)	0 (0%)
Taser	102	0 (0%)	0 (0%)
Total	568	72(13%)	221 (39%)

(This table was created by collapsing data from tables 4.1, 4.2, 4.3, and 4.4 from Meyer, 1992)

The Effectiveness of Tasers

Meyer (1992), in his study of LAPD use-of-force reports, discussed effectiveness rates for the individual weapons and techniques used. Meyer defined effectiveness as "if the application of force ended the altercation" (Meyer, 1992, p. 16). According to Meyer (1992), "there is overwhelming data to support the conclusions that non-lethal weapons are as effective as other force types, and that the use of selected non-lethal weapons results in virtually no serious injuries to officers or suspects" (p.16). The significance of this research is that it compares a variety of non-lethal use-of-force methods by a common set of standards, i.e., rate and severity of injuries and effectiveness.

The most-used types of force were the baton, the miscellaneous bodily force (pushing, shoving, grabbing), and the taser. The least-used force types were the chemical spray, flashlight, and punches. Meyer determined that the effectiveness rate of the baton was 85%, the "karate kick" effectiveness rate was 87%, the punch rate was 75%, and the miscellaneous force rate was 94%. The flashlight rate was 96% and the swarm, or organized tackle, rate was 92%. The chemical spray rate was 90% and the taser rate was 86%.

A similar study conducted in Henrico County, Virginia, examined a wide range of use-of-force methods for effectiveness. Using a self-reporting survey instrument, Smith and Petrocelli (2002) captured responses on the effectiveness of multiple use-of-force tactics employed by officers making arrests during 1999. The focus of this research was on the officers' use of a sequence of tactics to gain control of suspects. The significance of this research lies in validating the importance of officers progressing through multiple tactics to achieve higher levels of effectiveness.

A 2002 study by the Seattle Police Department (SPD) examined data on taser use by SPD during a 13-month period. The purposes of the study were to evaluate the effectiveness of the M26 taser as a LTL option for SPD officers and to identify any future training or deployment needs. The report concludes that the M26 Taser was effective in disabling offenders 92% of the time it was used, provided that verified taser contact was obtained. This occurred in only 85% of taser uses. The report documents that "Both officers and suspects reported low rates of injury during taser incidents when compared with other use-of-force situations" (SPD, 2002, p.3). A study by Hougland, Mesloh, and Henych, (2005) examined taser use at the Orange County, Florida, Sheriff's Office. The effect on civil litigation by taser deployments was one area of their examination. Their study also examined the frequency of taser use and at what level in the use-of-force matrix, or continuum, the taser was deployed. Their data indicates that, since being implemented, the taser became the primary LTL weapon deployed by officers. Despite the fact that agency policy allows for use at the passive resistance level of the Use-of-Force Continuum, the taser was deployed more often (69%) in situations when officers encountered active physical resistance (Hougland et al. 2005).

In one of the more recent studies, White and Ready (2007) examined the use of tasers in a large metropolitan police agency during a three year period. Their study examined 243 taser uses between 2002 and 2004. The findings of their study indicate that the taser was used almost exclusively on violent suspects classified as emotionally disturbed. Despite being used in encounters that are more violent the taser was found to be effective in 85% of cases. This study did not examine taser uses that resulted in serious injury or death.

Despite the fact that some commonalities exist in cases where deaths occur from taser use, it appears that more research is needed. Additional research is needed to clarify the standards to be used to measure the effects of the taser that may cause unintentional death or injury. A larger sampling of these types of cases should be reviewed to capture more of the variables affecting the analyses of the taser as a LTL weapon and to better assess the risks associated with its use.

Suspect Injuries and Unanticipated Consequences of Taser Use

There is a body of research that examines the effectiveness of tasers in rendering suspects compliant; however, there is limited medical research available on its effects on human subjects. A 1991 study conducted by the Chief Medical Examiner in Los Angeles County which examined sixteen deaths associated with taser use in Los Angeles County between 1983 and 1987 was reviewed (Kornblum, 1991). The study presented a general profile of the victims, their age, sex, and race. Also documented were specific behaviors exhibited when the police encountered them and the manner of death (accident or homicide). The study specifically looked at whether or not the suspect was found to be under the influence of illegal drugs, the time interval between the taser deployment and death, and the number of taser cassettes fired. According to Kornblum (1991), drugs, specifically cocaine, PCP, or amphetamines, were found in 13 of 16 cases. All of these subjects sustained some form of injuries varying from a few superficial abrasions to gunshot wounds. "...aside from the injuries sustained in the confrontation with police and the use of the taser, these deaths vary only slightly from those caused by solely cocaine or PCP" (p.445). This conclusion supports the position that the taser alone is not to blame for these injuries.

A review of the injuries related to the use of tasers by the Portland, Oregon, Police Department between June 2002 and July 2003 was conducted by McManus, Forsyth, Hawks, and Jui, (2004). This study revealed that 42 percent of 227 taser deployments generated EMS reports. During the study period, there were no documented dysrhythmias or cardiac complaints and sixty of the patients (63%) had no documented injury. Minor secondary injuries (hematomas, lacerations, and contusions) were documented in 27 (28%) of the patients. Nine (9%) of the patients sustained self-inflicted or unrelated injuries. McManus et al. (2004) concluded, "the M26 taser appears to be a safe and effective non-lethal weapon" (p. 587). Despite the fact that no deaths were reported during their examination, the authors note a higher incidence of injuries than manufacturer reports claim.

Ordog, Wasserberger, Schalater, and Balasubramanium (1987) examined 218 patients who were treated in an emergency room after being shot by police with a taser for violent or criminal behavior in Los Angeles County between July 1980 and December 1985. Their report found that complications associated with taser wounds included contusions, abrasions, and lacerations in 38 percent of the cases examined. Another 1 percent suffered mild rhabdomyolysis, or muscle breakdown, and a smaller (0.5) percent of suspects suffered testicular torsion. According to the report, "Although 48% of 'tasered' patients required hospitalization, all but one was for a preexisting injury or toxic or psychiatric problem" (p.78). The authors concluded that tasers are relatively safe when compared to more conventional weapons (Ordog et al., 1987).

A medical literature review conducted by Bleetman and Steyn (2003) concluded that the medical risks of electronic weaponry compare favorably with those of more conventional methods of controlling noncompliant and violent subjects. The risk factors for death in 'tasered' subjects appear to be no different from known risk factors for death in custody and include the subjects' use of drugs and symptoms, such as exhaustion or bizarre behavior, that lead to the arrest.

Despite the limited numbers of deployments of tasers by its police forces in the United Kingdom, some preliminary research into the use of tasers has taken place. A report by the United Kingdom's Defense Scientific Advisory Council's subcommittee concluded that the risk of life threatening or serious injuries from the M26 Advanced Taser appears to be very low (DOMILL, 2004). It should be noted that most police use of tasers in the UK are by special units within the Metropolitan Police Force, who are also equipped with firearms. This greatly influences the types of situations where tasers are deployed in an operational context (Lewer and Davison, 2006).

In the Taser Task Force (2005) study conducted by the Orange County Sheriff's Office in Orlando, Florida, a medical expert panel reviewed the medical literature offered by Taser International, Inc., and numerous other independent studies during their investigation of taser deployments by the Sheriff's Office over a 5-year period. "The panel concluded the level of electrical output or shock delivered by a taser is unlikely to cause serious or permanent injury". (OCSO Task Force, 2005, p.35).

An examination by Williams (2008) of 213 unexpected deaths from 1983 to 2005 in police custody, which followed a taser use, found that in 182 of the 212 cases the taser was excluded as the direct cause of death. In only two cases did the weight of evidence suggest that the taser was either the cause of death or a significant contributing factor.

One of the more comprehensive independent medical studies of injuries related to conducted electrical weapon (CEW), or taser use was conducted by Bozeman et al. (2009). This study examined 1,201 CEW uses by six different law enforcement agencies during a three-year period. The study found that less than 1% of the suspects in the examined cases suffered serious injuries.

In an attempt to mitigate injuries to suspects and to govern the use of tasers as a LTL weapon, police agencies have developed organizational policies that provide guidance on the prudent use of tasers. The placement of tasers in the Use-of-Force Continuum gives officers instruction on what level of suspect resistance must be present to authorize the deployment of the taser. The development and implementation of these policies regarding taser use represents a significant challenge for police administrators. The policies that govern taser use have also generated considerable public criticism and media scrutiny. As with any organizational policy that deals with high-liability areas of police activity, the issues that drive the policy change are often politically charged and force police leaders to confront difficult issues and make value judgments. A significant body of research deals specifically with the process and effect of policy change. A significant part of this study will examine the effect of policy change related to the use of taser and how it has effected taser use.

THE RESEARCH ON ORGANIZATIONAL POLICY CHANGE

Organizational change in police agencies has been the subject of a large body of work by various researchers. The majority of this work relates to macro structural changes in organizations and how they affect work performance, policy development, agency members' perceptions, and effectiveness (Guyot, 1979; King, 2003; Thacher and Rein, 2004).

Other researchers have focused on the paramilitary structure of police agencies and how it effects police organizational change (Auten; 1985; Crank and Langworthy, 1992; Rasor, 1999). Much of this research seeks to remedy the cultural resistance to change for police organizations. According to Lingamneni (1979), "Police organizations and the individuals which make up those organizations have tended to resist substantive changes recommended from both within and outside their ranks" (p.25). Thus, police often are very resistant to changes to either organizational structure or police procedures. This tendency leads to the development of policy in a variety of unorthodox and complex ways.

While police have always been enamored with tools and weapons, one of the areas where police have been resistant to change historically is the advent of new procedures, tactics, and policies that guide their use. Mosher (1967), in his work on government reorganizations, identified new technology, new equipment, and advancing knowledge as identifiable factors that make change necessary. Regardless of the impetus for change using new procedures and tactics, various researchers have attempted to understand why, when, and how policy does (or does not) change.

The dilemma faced by police officers when use of force is indicted is that, despite the placement of tasers in the Use-of-Force Continuum, the officers, because of their core value, conflict with trying to balance safety for all and, therefore, tend to use it when they see fit, even if this conflicts with agency policy. The testing of the officer's ability to balance these values with when to use this type of nonlethal force is the focus of this research study.

A THEORETICAL FRAMEWORK FOR ORGANIZATIONAL POLICY CHANGE

Thacher and Rein (2004) provide a theoretical framework for the study of the effects of policy change on taser use and effectiveness. Their theory of value conflict and policy change explicates government's tendency to balance competing goals or striking tradeoffs among values. They define values-oriented casuistry, or rationalization, as a form of moral taxonomy that aids in values balancing. Stewert (2006) interprets this theory further by explaining how "police departments, required to give their officers guidance on how to handle criminals effectively without undue harm, often come up with case-by-case approaches on how to respond to particular situations" (p. 184).

Taser use and the policies that guide its use must always attempt to balance competing values involving the safety of the public and suspects, as well as the safety of the police officer. The Use-of-Force Continuum provides an example of this values management casuistry. Therefore, the Use-of-Force Continuum and the policies that guide its use represent the police agencies' attempts to manage the conflict, thereby maintaining safety for all.

According to Thacher and Rein (2004) "policy actors eschew general decisions about how conflicting values should be weighed; instead, they encourage and facilitate case-by-case judgment about how decisions should be made, typically using analytical reasoning to do so" (p.464).

Many forms of decision-making in government can be seen as casuistic responses to problems of value choice, such as retirement policy, crime policy, and refugee policy. Policy on the use of force by police also clearly qualifies as one of these areas. The use of LTL weapons and the policies that guide their use attempt to "balance" the competing values of the public safety, including suspects or bystanders, and the safety of the police officer.

The Use-of-Force Continuum is a practical example of this values management casuistry. Bittner (1970) states that Use-of-Force Continuum guidelines are built upon the assertion that police coercion is, and must be, situationally justified. According to Terrill (2005), "Situations confronting officers may vary infinitely, but workable standards to be used on the street cannot mirror that level of complexity and are limited by the ... number of principles and categories" (p.110).

The continuum is taxonomy of appropriate levels of force to be used by officers confronted by suspect resistance or violence. These policies represent the balancing of values conflict. When making policy decisions, governments must weigh the risks versus the rewards of determining appropriate levels of authorized police force. The Use-of-Force Continuum and the policies that guide its use represent police policy makers' attempts to manage the conflict between these two competing values.

It is understood that police use of force is central to the police mission (Bittner, 1970, 1990). The appropriate proportional and incremental nature of that force is not as clear

(Klockars, 1996). The Use-of-Force Continuum is an incremental guide for police officers to employ when confronting noncompliant or resistive suspects. The movement of levels of force up or down the continuum is a subjective decision based on many situational factors. Most of these factors are external to the bureaucratic police-working environment. These can include the suspect's demeanor, the degree of danger to the officer, or the presence of a weapon. The internal working environment is often referred to as the degree of license given to police officers to use force (White, 2001). Police policy makers must apply a reasonableness standard as interpreted by state and federal laws when creating or amending agency policies. Often, it is this application of reasonableness that leads to a values balancing by policy makers. This balancing typically comes in the form of implementing new policy or amending existing policies.

Thacher and Rein (2004) cite noted police scholar Carl Klockars, who discusses in great detail the dilemma faced by police decision makers who must manage the use of force by police applying the nebulous definitions of excessive or appropriate levels of force provided by constitutional lawmakers (Klockars, 1996). It is these laws that predominantly must guide policy development on police use of force. The question ultimately becomes "How can society authorize the use of necessary force but eliminate the use of excessive force?" (Thacher and Rein, 2004, p. 477).

Much of the controversy surrounding taser use relates to the frequency of its use and the specific situations when police officers should use it, which is governed by the Use-of-Force Continuum (Adams and Jennison, 2007). The influence of external political forces on policymaking is a central concern for policy change theorists. What is not clear is the role public scrutiny of police actions plays in motivating and influencing the policy change or the effect on officers' actions and perceptions. This study will explore these questions by examining an organizational policy change related to police use of force. This change raised the level of suspect resistance required to justify the use of the taser. By examining archival data and officer survey responses, this study will evaluate the effect of policy change on taser deployments.

This policy change was made ostensibly to limit the use of tasers on suspects who were only passively resisting the actions of officers. Passive resistance is defined as refusing to comply with the commands of officers but not offering physical resistance. The policy change was also an attempt to mitigate injuries to suspects in lower intensity encounters. It was also made at a time of significant public and media scrutiny of taser use and the injuries inflicted during deployments. The intent of the policy makers was to balance the need to protect citizens and officers' safety while still maintaining order. This is a practical example of "striking tradeoffs" or the values balancing that Thacher and Rein (2004) discuss in their theory on organizational policy change.

Weighing the need to protect life but also preserve order is a cornerstone of the police mission. This study uses Thacher and Rein's (2004) theory as a framework for understanding if the policy change relating to taser placement on the Use-of-Force Continuum achieved the theoretical balancing described in their values-oriented casuistry of the need to protect officers but not unnecessarily risk injuries to suspects. Clearly more explicit testing is necessary to quantitatively prove or disprove this theoretical framework.

SUMMARY AND CONCLUSIONS

The data that is available on the use of tasers by police suggests that taser use is beneficial at controlling noncompliant suspects, without inflicting serious injury, and rarely has its use resulted in death. A review of current literature supports the effectiveness of taser use although there are no current studies that examine the effect that use-of-force organizational policy changes can have on taser use. Much of the public controversy surrounding tasers focuses on when and how often officers should deploy them (PERF, 2005).

In an attempt to mitigate public concerns and guide officers on the proper use of tasers, many agencies have changed their policies on placement of the taser on the Use-of-Force Continuum based on the level of suspect resistance encountered. This has been done by raising the level of suspect resistance required to authorize the use of tasers in a use of force encounter. The effect of these policy changes on overall taser use has never been quantitatively evaluated or measured. This research is designed to provide quantifiable evidence to explicate these questions. Further research in this area can help to instill public confidence in law enforcement's ability to maintain order without inflicting unnecessary injuries to suspects.

Various studies have been conducted on the use of tasers by police and their effectiveness as a LTL use-of-force method. To date, there are no studies that focus on organizational policy and how a change in taser placement on the Use-of-Force Continuum influences taser use and effectiveness. This study will examine one police agency's taser use after a change in policy designed to mitigate its use. The information gathered from this study will help to bridge the gap between previous studies that have focused primarily on specific factors, such as civil litigation, harm to suspects, and officer injuries. This study will examine the use of tasers during police-citizen encounters using use-of-force incident data to see how a change in organizational policy has affected its deployment and how this core value conflict plays into this nexus. This study will also use a survey instrument to gather responses from taser users related to their perceptions and experiences with taser use.

A thorough review of the literature reveals that anecdotal data exists that suggests that taser usage is beneficial in preventing serious injury to suspects or officers and rarely has its use resulted in death (Bozeman et al. 2009; Fish and Geddes, 2001; Hamilton, 1991; Kornblum, 1991; Meyer, 1992; Nielson, 2001). What is needed in the literature are more studies that examine how organizational policy changes related to its placement on the Use-of-Force Continuum can alter the effectiveness of taser use.

Taser manufacturers have begun to market these weapons aggressively in the lay community. One company, Taser International, has begun selling tasers to women by showcasing them at home taser parties in much the same way as Tupperware products are marketed and sold (The Associated Press, 2008). This trend, coupled with the increasing influence of these weapons on the police mission, all but ensures that the current level of public scrutiny of their use will continue. The media attention that recent injuries and deaths have drawn has also fueled the controversy. Research into the effectiveness of taser use and organizational policy changes could resolve many of the questions surrounding its use by police. Additional research will give police administrators and the public information needed to make informed decisions on the prudent use of public funds for these weapons. Further research will provide guidance to police on policy development related to the taser. This research could also help to instill greater public confidence in law enforcement's ability to maintain order without inflicting unintended harm to suspects or officers.

CHAPTER THREE:
Examining Taser Use in One Police Agency

This work examines the effect of organizational policy changes regarding the placement of the taser on the Use-of-Force Continuum on taser deployments. Officers' perceptions of taser effectiveness after the policy change were also examined. The question explored in this study is whether there is a relationship between officer attitudes related to taser use and their subsequent perception of taser effectiveness.

This study examines one agency's experiences with tasers during two separate time periods, using archival use of force and officer survey data. This examination is crucial as much of the debate and controversy regarding the use of tasers by police focuses on the circumstances surrounding when police use tasers and what level of suspect resistance it is designed to defeat (Cronin and Ederheimer, 2006). After the introduction of newer and more powerful tasers in the early 1980s, many police agencies integrated their deployment into the Use-of-Force Continuum at a level to be used when suspects were only passively resisting the actions of the officer. The use of tasers in these low- intensity situations led to considerable media attention and public controversy (PERF, 2005). A review of current literature reveals no empirical research on the placement of tasers into the Use-of-Force Continuum. In response to this scrutiny and to mitigate citizen complaints, many police agencies increased the required level of resistance by suspects from passive resistance to active physical resistance before tasers were authorized to be deployed. To date, no research studies have been conducted that examine this change in use-of-force policy to determine the effect it has had on taser deployments.

For purposes of comparison, taser use-of-force data from two separate time periods was examined. Use of force data from the period before the change in policy to a higher level of force comprises the first data set for analysis. The second set of archival data examines data after the change in policy to determine what effect, if any, the change had on several identified areas. Survey data from actual taser users was collected to capture officer perceptions of organizational change. This survey data was examined and compared to use-of-force forms to determine if officer's perceptions and the gathered archival data reflect similar patterns and findings. The literature generates the research questions and hypotheses listed below.

Research Questions

Research Question 1: What effect has raising the authorized level on the Use-of-Force Continuum for taser deployment had on the frequency of taser deployments?

Research Question 2: What effect has raising the authorized level on the Use-of-Force Continuum for taser deployment had on the level of suspect resistance encountered by officers?

Research Question 3: What effect has raising the authorized level on the Use-of-Force Continuum for taser deployment had on the frequency of injuries to suspects from taser deployments?

Research Question 4: What effect has raising the authorized level on the Use-of-Force Continuum for taser deployment had on the severity of injuries to suspects from taser deployments?

Research Question 5: What effect has raising the authorized level on the Use-of-Force Continuum for taser deployment had on the frequency of injuries to officers during taser deployments?

Research Question 6: Do officers report that the change in organizational policy on the authorized level regarding the Use-of-Force Continuum, which outlines when the taser can be deployed, has increased the risk of harm to them in a use-of-force encounter?

Research Question 7: Do officers perceive that the change in organizational policy relating to the authorized level on the Use-of-Force Continuum, when the taser can be used, has increased the risk of harm to suspects in a use-of-force encounter?

Research Question 8: Do officers perceive that raising the authorized level on the Use-of-Force Continuum for taser deployment places the taser at an appropriate level of force for most encounters?

DATA

This study uses two sources of data: (1) agency use-of-force archival data and (2) survey data from taser-equipped officers. The archival data were gathered from the Orlando Police Department (OPD) during two separate 12-month periods. The purpose of this examination is to analyze the effect on the frequency of taser deployments, injuries to suspects, injuries to officers and levels of suspect resistance after changes in organizational policy that altered the placement of tasers on the Use-of-Force Continuum.

The OPD in Orlando, Florida, was selected as the site for this research because of its size, the length of time tasers have been in use, and the fact that the agency changed its policy regarding placement of the taser on the Use-of-Force Continuum.

The OPD staffing as of 2005 is approximately 706 sworn police officers, or 3.2 officers per 1,000 residents. The Police Chief is appointed by the Mayor, who is an elected official. The City of Orlando occupies approximately 110 square miles and is located in Central Florida. The population in 2005 was 217,567 residents with a daily service population of approximately

320,000. The City of Orlando has experienced significant growth from 1996 to 2005 with the population increasing 17% or by 44,445 new residents during that period. Orlando is also one of the most popular tourist destinations in the world, with 36 million people a year visiting the area's theme parks and attractions.

In 2005, the violent crime rate in Orlando was 17.47 incidents per 1,000 residents. The rate of property crime per 1,000 residents was 83.77 (FDLE, 2005). Data on the population, the changes in population between 1996 and 2005, the reported crime rate, and the fluctuation of crime rates over time for the City of Orlando was examined.

Several other major cities in Florida were also examined and comparisons were made in a variety of categories to determine how Orlando compares with other similar sized metropolitan cities. This data supports that in a majority of these categories, which measure growth, crime rates and police service delivery measures, the City of Orlando compares favorably with that of other major cities in Florida (See Table 4).

In January 2001, OPD adopted the taser as a less-than-lethal alternative. To date, approximately 700 tasers have been issued to police officers. The OPD also equips their officers with OC Chemical Spray and ASP expandable batons as less-than-lethal use-of-force alternatives.

The OPD requires the completion of a defensive tactics form by the first-line supervisor after each taser deployment (See Appendix B). The content of the form is reviewed by multiple managers, and copies are sent to the Internal Affairs and Training sections. The use-of-force report form requires the supervisor to document the level of resistance offered by the suspect and the level of force used to compel the suspect into compliance. Additional demographic information on these forms includes the officer's name, age, and tenure with the agency. Demographic information about the suspect is also captured, including name, race, sex, date of birth, home address, and physical condition prior to the incident.

Table 4: Florida Police Department Comparison

Police Department	Orlando	Miami	Tampa	St. Petersburg	Ft. Lauderdale	Hollywood
Square Miles Served (2006)	110	35.7	112.1	59.6	31.7	27.3
1996:						
Population Served	173,122	365,127	289,337	241,276	150,150	125,689
Crime Rate per 100,000	13,895	14,493	14,817	10,016	16,972	9,973
Total Crime Index	24,055	52,918	42,871	24,165	25,484	12,535
Homicides	13	124	41	24	31	10
Robberies	1,080	5,139	2,671	1,371	1,186	502
Violent Crime per 1,000	23.17	32.84	30.02	22.65	17.19	9.21
Property Crime per 1,000	115.83	112.09	118.15	77.50	152.53	90.52
2000:						
Population Served	185,951	362,470	303,447	248,232	152,397	139,357
Crime Rate per 100,000	12,030	10,968	11,095	8,220	8,387	6,900
Total Crime Index	22,369	39,756	33,666	20,404	12,782	9,616
Homicides	21	66	38	14	13	3
Robberies	1,044	3,077	2,183	990	760	424
Violent Crime per 1,000	21.11	21.73	21.03	16.23	11.56	7.76
Property Crime per 1,000	99.18	87.95	89.92	65.97	72.31	61.25

Table 4, cont.

Police Department	Orlando	Miami	Tampa	St. Petersburg	Ft. Lauderdale	Hollywood
2005:						
Population Served	217,567	386,882	326,519	253,902	171,344	143,025
Crime Rate per 100,000	10,124	7,613	7,650	7,980	7,423	5,084
Total Crime Index	22,027	29,455	24,978	20,260	12,719	7,271
Homicides	22	54	20	30	15	6
Robberies	1,204	2,019	1,160	959	741	330
Violent Crime per 1,000	17.47	15.84	14.42	15.51	8.77	5.40
Property Crime per 1,000	83.77	58.88	62.08	64.29	65.46	45.43
Sworn Officers	706	1,103	984	552	454	326
Sworn per 1,000	3.2	2.64	3.02	2.18	2.65	2.28

Sources: FDLE Total Index Crime for Florida, Jurisdiction and Offense, 1996, 2000, 2005

Violent crime – homicide, forcible rape, robbery, aggravated assault

Property crime – burglary, larceny, motor vehicle theft)

Sworn officer data FDLE 2005, Criminal Justice Agency Profile

Several situational variables are also required on the form. These include whether the suspect was intoxicated; if the suspect had prior or new injuries; if medical treatment was required; the incident type; the date, time, and physical location of the incident; the number of involved officers; and the presence of citizen bystanders.

Survey data was also used to examine the perceptions of officers related to the effect of the change in organizational policy on taser deployments. The officers surveyed were selected from a sample of taser-equipped officers. The officers were identified through the examination of the archival data, and they must have used a taser during both of the time periods examined in this study.

PROCEDURES FOR EXAMINING ARCHIVAL DATA

Archival taser use data for the June 4, 2003 through June 3, 2004 (Pretest) and June 5, 2004 through June 5, 2005 (Posttest) time periods were compared. These data collection dates reflect the timetable for implementing the change in agency policy that requires officers to use the taser only when the encounter involves active physical resistance, on their Use-of-Force Continuum. This organizational policy change took place on June 4, 2004 for the OPD (see Figure 1).

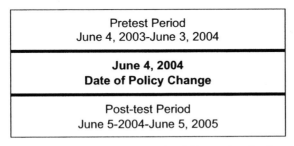

| Pretest Period |
| June 4, 2003-June 3, 2004 |
| **June 4, 2004** |
| **Date of Policy Change** |
| Post-test Period |
| June 5-2004-June 5, 2005 |

Figure 1: Timeline for Archival Data Analysis

These data collection time periods capture use-of-force incidents that occurred one year before and one year after the organizational policy change regarding taser placement in the Use-of-Force Continuum. OPD officers are guided on the use of tasers, also listed as electronic control devices (ECD)[1], by agency policy 1128.6, which governs the use of force by Orlando Police Officers. The policy contains a resistance and response continuum that consists of six levels of resistance: indicators of resistance, verbal resistance, passive resistance, active resistance, aggressive resistance, and deadly force resistance (see Appendix A). The continuum also lists employee's response levels, which coincide with suspect resistance. These include employee presence, verbal directions, soft control, hard control, intensified techniques, and deadly force. Within each response level on the form are required fields that denote specifically which weapon or technique the officer deployed.

The OPD requires the officer's supervisor to complete the use-of-force form if the suspect required medical treatment or was admitted to or treated and released from the hospital. A narrative portion requires the supervisor to describe the resistance offered and the suspect's specific actions. There is also a portion requiring supervisory comments on the use of force, and the form must be signed by each level of the officer's chain of command. The form must also be attached to a copy of the agency incident report, which is completed for each incident.

PROCEDURES FOR ADMINISTERING SURVEY INSTRUMENT

A survey instrument for capturing officer perceptions of the effect of the policy changes on taser deployments was developed (See Appendix C). Prior to administering the survey instrument to the selected sample of officers, a pretest sample of three officers from OPD and two deputies from the Orange County Sheriff's Office were asked to take the survey and comment on its clarity and ease of completion. Feedback was obtained from each of these participants and changes were made to the survey

---

[1] The Orlando Police department uses the term (ECD) electronic control devices to describe tasers. This term is used interchangeably throughout this document.

instrument. The majority of their comments pertained to the length of the instrument and recommended changes in wording to some of the questions. This process was done to guarantee that the content validity of the survey was maintained (Babbie, 2001).

The revised instrument was then administered to a sample of 333 OPD officers. The officers chosen to participate in the survey were identified by examining the archival use-of-force data and selecting officers who deployed tasers during both the pre and posttest periods. Only those officers who deployed a taser during these time periods and who were still employed by the OPD were chosen to participate in the survey.

University of Central Florida Institutional Review Board (IRB) approval was obtained in June 2007 (See Appendix D). The survey instrument was administered via electronic mail using Internet-based survey software that delivered the survey instrument to the officers at their agency e-mail addresses. This method was chosen because this is the customary way for Orlando police officers to receive agency information and correspondence. This also was used to improve the response rate and the quality of responses. The identities of the respondents are known only to the researcher and will not be divulged. Respondents were provided access to the survey software through an online Web site link for an eight-week period, beginning July 7, 2007 and ending September 1, 2007.

The recipients were provided several opportunities to participate in the survey. The survey instrument was originally sent to recipients on July 7, 2007. A second message with the survey Web site link was sent on August 1, 2007 to those recipients who had not previously responded, and a final reminder message was sent to any additional recipients that had not responded on August 21, 2007. Once officers submitted their responses to the survey instrument, they could no longer access the web site. No surveys were received after August 27, 2007. A timeline is presented in Table 5 to depict when surveys were received.

Table 5: Timeline of Receipt of Survey Responses

Date that Surveys were Received	Total Number of Surveys Received	% of Surveys Received
July 7, 2007 – August 1,2007	104	73%
August 2, 2007 – August 21, 2007	27	19%
August 22, 2007 – September 1, 2007	12	8%
Total	**143***	**100%**

* 13 surveys were excluded from the sample due to missing data leaving the survey sample at 130.

The survey instrument consisted of an informed consent form and forty questions that captured officers' perceptions of how the change in organizational policy relating to taser placement on the Use-of-Force Continuum has effected their safety and the safety of suspects in use-of-force encounters. The survey also captured the officers' demographic information, such as education level; job assignments during the archival data study period; rank during the test periods; agency tenure; and previous employment in law enforcement. A variety of subject areas, such as risk of injury to suspects, risk of injury to officers, the proper placement . of the taser on the Use-of-Force Continuum and the effectiveness of the taser in subduing noncompliant or combative suspects were examined using officer survey responses.

To assist the reader in understanding the composition of officers who were surveyed, Table 6 illustrates the comparisons between the survey sample, the sampling frame and the population of officers employed by the Orlando Police Department. An analysis of these data reveals that the survey sample contained responses from 11 (8.5%) Black officers, 99 (76.2%) White officers, 14 (10.8%) Hispanic officers, 4 (3.1%) Asian officers, and 6 (4.7%) Native American or other officers. The demographics of the Orlando Police Department are 137 (18.9%) Black officers, 454 (62.8%) White officers, 107 (14.8%) Hispanic officers, 21 (2.9%) Asian officers, and 4 (.6 %) Native American or other officers. These data and the officer demographics from the archival use of force data and OPD are presented in Table 6.

Data on similar sized police agencies was also examined. Using data provided by the United States Department of Justice Law Enforcement Management and Administrative Statistics survey (LEMAS) (2003) a comparison with the data from OPD was conducted. The officer racial and gender demographics of police agencies that serve populations from 100,000-249,999 are as follows: Black (11.9%), White (76.0%), Hispanic/Latino (9.1%), and Other[2] (3.0%). The percentage of officers by gender is 89.0 % male and 11.0% female. This examination revealed that OPD employs more Black and Hispanic officers and fewer White officers than the national average for cities of similar size. The numbers of Asian and Other officers were comparable. The percentage of female officers is also slightly higher than the national average for similar sized agencies.

Table 6: Sample Demographic Comparisons

Variable	Value Labels	Survey Sample		Force Population		OPD Population	
		N	%	N	%	N	%
Race of Officer	Black	11	8.5	66	19.8	137	18.9
	White	99	76.7	229	68.8	454	62.8
	Hispanic	14	10.9	24	7.2	107	14.8
	Asian/Other	5	3.9	14	4.2	25	3.5
		129	**100.0**	**333**	**100.0**	**723**	**100.0**
Gender of Officer	Male	119	91.5	293	87.9	606	83.9
	Female	11	8.5	40	12.1	117	16.1
		130	**100.0**	**333**	**100.0**	**723**	**100.**

As shown in Table 6, Black officers were less likely than expected to respond to the survey. Similarly, white officers appeared to respond more often than the sampling frame would predict. In order to test if there are significant differences in

---

[2] The other category includes Asians, Native Hawaiians, or other Pacific Islanders, American Indians, Alaska Natives, and any other race.

these key demographic variables a chi-square test was run on these key demographic variables. This test is important to make sure that the respondents chosen match or are at least representative of the population sampled. In this case, since the sampling frame was officers from OPD, that used a taser in this time period. Comparisons are also made between the survey sample and those that used force during the archival data period and the entire population of OPD officers. The first comparison tells us if there is a representative sample. The second comparison examines how well the sampling frame compares to the larger population of officers employed by OPD. In addition, the final comparison examines how well the sample compared to OPD in general. While each of these comparisons shed light on the sample, the critical one is the initial test that compares the sample to the sample of officers who used force.

Table 7: Chi-Square Test for Difference in Populations of Officers in Opposing Samples

Variable	Samples Compared	Chi Square	Sig.	*df*
Race	Survey Sample to Force Population	9.47*	.024	3
	Force Population to OPD	12.29*	.006	3
	Survey to OPD	11.38*	.007	3
Gender	Survey Sample to Force Population	1.2	.272	1
	Force Population to OPD	3.13	.076	1
	Survey to OPD	5.15*	.023	1

* Difference is significant at the .05 for a two tailed test

As shown in Table 7, there are significant race differences between each of the populations. It appears that since fewer blacks and more whites responded to the survey this would indicate a possible problem with the representativeness of the sample. However, when the gender composition of the samples is examined, there is no difference between the survey sample and the sampling frame, for the sampling frame and the population of OPD. The only difference is between the survey sample and the general population of officers employed by OPD. This difference is likely the result of the difference in the overall population sizes between these two samples and the way a chi square test calculates the differences in the frequency expected for each cell.

Despite finding that there is a difference in the racial composition between the three samples and a difference in the gender composure between the sample and the general population of officers employed by OPD, the chi square test tells us little about where the differences occur. A cursory examination of Table 6 shows where these differences are likely to be (black and white). To confirm this casual observation, a Z-test for the differences in proportions was conducted. The results are depicted in Table 8.

Table 8: Z-Test for Difference in Proportions of Officers in Opposing Samples

Variable	Variable Label	Survey to Force Population		Force Population to OPD		Survey to OPD	
		Z	Sig.	Z	Sig.	Z	Sig.
Race	Black	-2.92*	.003	.333	.738	-2.88*	.004
	White	1.69	.090	1.857	.059	3.058*	.002
	Hispanic	1.27	.200	-3.48*	.000	-1.18	.236
	Asian/Other	.159	.873	.598	.550	.237	.812
Gender	Male/Female	1.10	.272	1.77	.076	2.27*	.023

* Difference is significant at the .05 for a two-tailed test.

The Z test for the difference in proportions extends the chi-square test analysis by examining specific categories and identifying exactly where there is a difference. As shown in Table 8, this test ($z=-2.92$, $p=.003$) statistically confirms that black officers were underrepresented in the survey sample compared to the sampling frame. This is an issue that needs further discussion. While blacks responded to the survey less often than would be expected given the sampling frame and which raises questions regarding the representativeness of the sample, it does not mean that the survey results cannot be used.

The extant literature on the use of force is fairly consistent in finding that not only are black officers more likely to be deployed in areas where force is used more often, but they also use force on average more often than whites (Alpert, Dunham and MacDonald, 2004; Friedrich, 1980; Fyfe, 1979, 1987, Reiss, 1971). While this literature has not been extended into the use of taser per se, we can infer that it is likely that if black officers use force more often, then it is likely that they will also be more accepting of a wide variety of force options including the use of tasers. In fact, when looking at the basic demographics of officers who used tasers, 15 percent of the force situations involved black officers in the pre-test and 21 percent of these same incidents involved this group in the post test. Further, blacks only comprised 8.5 percent of the survey sample and 19.8 percent of officers that were in the sampling frame who used force. What shows is that black officers apparently used tasers more often than expected. Using this logic, it is likely that despite the fact that fewer black officers responded to the survey, the survey results may in all likelihood be a conservative estimate of the true opinion of officers because black officers may be more approving than their white, Hispanic or Asian peers. This however is an open empirical question and one that needs to be addressed by future research.

A review of data comparing officers who used taser to the officers at OPD reveals that there were fewer Hispanic officers who used tasers than expected. This finding may indicate that these officers were assigned in different places within the police department and had less opportunity to use tasers. The analysis comparing the survey respondents to all OPD officers reveals that there are fewer black officers, and more white officers that responded than one would expect just by looking at the racial composition of OPD.

An analysis of officer gender between the three groups was also conducted. There are no difference in gender between the survey sample and the force population ($z=1.10$, $p=.272$), nor is there any difference between the officers who used force and OPD ($z=1.77$, $p=.076$). However, there is a difference in the gender composition of survey respondents and OPD ($z=2.27$, $p=.023$). This difference can be explained because only officers who used a taser in this time period were sampled and it does not appear that female officers used them as often as male officers.

RESEARCH DESIGN

Study Variables Archival Data

This explanatory research design identifies the independent variable as the change in organizational policy on taser use. The dependent variables are the frequency of taser deployments; the level (severity) of suspect resistance encountered by officers; the frequency of suspect injuries; the severity of suspect injuries; and the frequency of officer injuries related to taser use. Table 9 provides definitions for these dependent variables.

Table 9: Definitions of Study Variables—Archival Data

Variable Name	Variable Type	Description	Data Source
Taser frequency before policy change	Continuous	Total number of taser deployments during the specified period/total # of arrests	Pre-existing data/defensive tactics forms
Taser frequency after policy change	Continuous	Total number of taser deployments during the specified period/ total # of arrests	Pre-existing data/ defensive tactics forms
Suspect resistance to taser before policy change	Ordinal	1 passive resistance 2 active physical resistance 3 aggressive physical resistance 4 deadly force resistance	Pre-existing data/ defensive tactics forms
Suspect resistance to taser after policy change	Ordinal	1 passive resistance 2 active physical resistance 3 aggressive physical resistance 4 deadly force resistance	Pre-existing data/ defensive tactics forms

Table 9, cont.

Variable Name	Variable Type	Description	Data Source
Officer injured before policy change	Dichotomous	0 no injury 1 injury	Pre-existing data/ defensive tactics forms
Officer injured after policy change	Dichotomous	0 no injury 1 injury	Pre-existing data/ defensive tactics forms
Suspect injured before policy change	Dichotomous	0 no injury 1 injury	Pre-existing data/ defensive tactics forms
Suspect injured after policy change	Dichotomous	0 no injury 1 injury	Pre-existing data/ defensive tactics forms
Severity of suspect injury	Interval	1 no injuries 2 standard injuries 3 abrasions, scratches 4 lacerations 5 hospital treatment required	Pre-existing data/ defensive tactics forms

Study Variables Survey Data

The study variables relating to the survey instrument capture officer perceptions in a variety of subject areas related to the effect of the policy change on the risk of injury to suspects, the risk of injury to officers, the proper taser placement on the Use-of-Force Continuum, and the effectiveness of the taser in subduing noncompliant or combative suspects. Table 10 provides definitions for these specific variables.

Table 10: Definitions of Study Variables—Survey Data

Variable Name	Variable Type	Description	Data Source
Officer perception—increased risk to officer after policy change	Ordinal	1 Strongly Disagree 2 Disagree Somewhat 3 Uncertain 4 Agree Somewhat 5 Strongly Agree	Officer Survey responses
Officer perception—proper placement of taser on Use-of-Force Continuum	Ordinal	1 Strongly Disagree 2 Disagree Somewhat 3 Uncertain 4 Agree Somewhat 5 Strongly Agree	Officer Survey responses
Officer perception—decreased frequency of taser use after policy change	Ordinal	1 Strongly Disagree 2 Disagree Somewhat 3 Uncertain 4 Agree Somewhat 5 Strongly Agree	Officer Survey responses
Officer perception—less able to control suspects after policy change	Ordinal	1 Strongly Disagree 2 Disagree Somewhat 3 Uncertain 4 Agree Somewhat 5 Strongly Agree	Officer Survey responses
Officer perception—placement of OC at level 4 appropriate for most use-of-force encounters	Ordinal	1 Strongly Disagree 2 Disagree Somewhat 3 Uncertain 4 Agree Somewhat 5 Strongly Agree	Officer Survey responses

CONTROL VARIABLES

Control variables for this study are situational level variables obtained from the use-of-force encounters. These include suspect age, sex, and race; the number of other officers present during the encounter; the presence of citizen bystanders; the seriousness of the encounter; and whether or not the incident was a call for service: or a self-initiated contact. These variables are consistent with research designs used in other studies of police use of force (Riksheim and Chermak, 1993; Terrill and Mastrofski, 2002). Table 11 provides definitions for these control variables.

Table 11: Definitions of Control Variables

Variable Name	Variable Type	Description	Data Source
Suspect race	Nominal	1 Black 2 White 3 Hispanic 4 Asian 5 Other	Pre-existing data/ defensive tactics forms
Suspect gender	Nominal	1 male 0 female	Pre-existing data/ defensive tactics forms
Suspect age	Interval	1 under 12 2 13-17 3 18-20 4 21-29 5 30-44 6 45-59 7 60+	Pre-existing data/ defensive tactics forms
Number of officers present	Interval	1 one 2 two 3 three 4 four 5 more than four	Pre-existing data/ defensive tactics forms
Number of citizen bystanders	Interval	0 none 1 one 2 two 3 three 4 four 5 more than four	Pre-existing data/ defensive tactics forms
The type of incident that led to the use-of-force encounter	Interval	1 Low threat 2 Medium threat 3 High threat	Pre-existing data/ defensive tactics forms
Officer-initiated or call for police service	Dichotomous	1 Self initiated by officer 0 Call for police service	Pre-existing data/ defensive tactics forms

ANALYSIS OF THE DATA

The unit of analysis for this study is use-of-force encounters. Existing use-of-force data was examined to form data sets in each of the identified categories. The research questions were addressed by first determining the types and frequencies of the force levels employed and resistance levels encountered in each incident. This strategy is consistent with research designs employed by Croft (1985), Meyer (1992), McLaughlin (1992) and Garner et al. (1996).

This analysis examined two separate sets of data to determine if the change in organizational policy had an effect on taser use and the outcomes of the encounter. The first data set was archival in nature and was coded directly from the use-of-force forms maintained by the OPD. The second data set was a survey consisting of multiple questions designed to see if the perceptions of officers matched the reality of actual use. These data sets are explained more fully in Chapter 4. A summary of statistical methods used to analyze the data is presented in the following paragraph.

The Z Test For The Differences in Two Proportions

The Z test for the differences in two proportions is designed to determine whether there is a difference between two population proportions and whether one is larger than the other. This test was applied to the data for the frequency of taser use in the pretest and posttest groups. To test the null hypothesis that the two proportions are equal a two-tailed test is used. A one-tailed test is used when trying to determine if one proportion is greater (or lower) than another (Weisburd, 1998).

Chi Square Tests

The Pearson's Chi square test is a nonparametric statistical test that seeks to determine if two or more variables are distributed equally. This statistic is used to test the hypothesis of no association of the identified variable data (Norušis, 2005). Chi square testing was done on the research questions relating to the frequency of injuries to suspects and the frequency of injuries to officers. These questions both use nominal level variables. This testing method also was applied to certain nominal-level individual and situational variables.

Independent Samples *T*-Test

An independent samples *t*-test is used to compare the mean scores of two different groups of people or conditions to determine if there is a significant difference between the groups. Independent samples t tests were conducted on the research questions relating to the levels of suspect resistance and the severity of injuries to suspects (Norušis, 2005). Both of these variables were treated as interval-level variables consistent with the framework laid out by Menard (1995). Menard claims that categorical variables such as Likert scales can be treated as interval level data if: (a) people believe them to be interval; (b) there is a true ordering to the data; (c) you have more than two categories and (d) the data are normally distributed. This testing method also was applied to certain interval-level individual and situational variables.

Ordinary Least Squares Regression

Ordinary Least Squares (OLS) Regression were applied to the research questions relating to the levels of suspect resistance and the severity of injuries to suspects, both of which were treated as interval-level variables. The use of the regression test extends the bivariate analysis already provided by t tests. This test allows for identifying when a change in the nature or direction of the relationship occurs when the effects of significant variables are controlled (Menard, 1995; Schroeder et al, 1986; Tabachnick and Fidell, 1996).

SUMMARY AND CONCLUSIONS

The purpose of this work is to examine the effect of organizational policy changes regarding the placement of the taser on the Use-of-Force Continuum on deployments and officer's perceptions of taser effectiveness. Officers' perceptions of taser effectiveness after the change in placement for authorized taser use on the Use-of-Force Continuum were also examined. The question explored in this study is whether there is a relationship between officer attitudes related to the use of force regarding the taser and their subsequent perception of taser effectiveness. This study examines one agency's experiences with tasers during two separate time periods, using archival use of force and officer survey data.

This study uses two sources of data: (1) agency use-of-force archival data and (2) survey data from taser-equipped officers. The archival data were gathered from the Orlando Police Department (OPD) during two separate 12-month periods. These data collection time periods capture use-of-force incidents that occurred one year before and one year after the organizational policy change regarding taser placement in the Use-of-Force Continuum. The OPD in Orlando, Florida, was selected as the site for this research because of its size, the length of time tasers have been in use, and the fact that the agency changed its policy regarding placement of the taser on the Use-of-Force Continuum. OPD compares favorably with other large metropolitan police agencies of similar size and composition.

Use of force data from OPD before the change in policy to a higher level of force comprises the first data set for analysis. The second set of archival data examines data after the change in policy to determine what effect, if any, the change had on several identified areas. Survey data from actual taser users was collected to capture officer perceptions of the effect on taser use after the organizational change. This survey data was examined and compared to use-of-force forms to determine if officer's perceptions and the gathered archival data reflect similar patterns and findings.

Survey data was also used to examine the perceptions of officers related to the effect of the change in organizational policy on taser deployments. The officers surveyed were selected from a sample of taser-equipped officers. These officers were identified through the examination of the archival data, and they must have used a taser during both of the time periods examined in this study.

This chapter has described the methodology and research plan for this study, including the examination of use-of-force forms to capture archival data, the development of the survey instrument, the selection of the survey recipients, and the plan for distribution of the survey to officers. Chapter 4 describes the data used in this study, both from archival use-of-force data and data acquired through the user survey. In addition, Chapter 4 reports on the analyses of these data in the empirical tests of this study's hypotheses.

CHAPTER FOUR:

Research Study Findings

SIGNIFICANCE OF THE CURRENT RESEARCH FINDINGS

The use of tasers by police has been the subject of considerable debate and scrutiny since their introduction as a less-than-lethal weapon in the late 1970s (IACP, 2004). This controversy has been revitalized with the introduction of a newer generation of weapons in the late 1990s (Cronin and Ederheimer, 2006; McBride and Tedder, 2005). These weapons are more powerful and have been deployed extensively by police agencies across the United States and abroad. There is a limited body of research on the use and effects of tasers. The majority of this research focuses on the effectiveness of tasers and how frequently they are deployed in use-of-force encounters. A review of current literature reveals no empirical research on the placement of tasers in the Use-of-Force Continuum. Additionally, no research studies have been conducted that examine this change in use-of-force policy to determine its effect on taser deployments or officers' attitudes related to taser effectiveness.

This study attempts to fill this void by examining taser use prior to, and after the implementation of, a policy change on taser placement in the Use-of-Force Continuum. In practice, it is obvious that police leaders have attempted to mitigate and manage the use of tasers by modifying organizational policies particularly related to high-risk situations to protect officers or suspects. The mechanism that most police agencies use to guide officers in use-of-force encounters is the Use-of-Force Continuum (Conner, 1991).

The purpose of this research study is to examine the effects of an organizational policy change that alters the taser placement in the

Use-of-Force Continuum. Using archival use-of-force and survey data, this study examines one agency's experiences with tasers during two separate time periods. The period one year before the organizational change in policy that altered the placement of the taser on the resistance and response continuum to a higher level of resistance will comprise the first data set for analysis3. The second set of archival data examines data one year after the policy change to determine what effect, if any, the change had on several identified variables. To attempt to capture officer perceptions of organizational change, survey data from taser users was also collected. This data will be examined to determine if officers' perceptions and actual taser use statistics reflect similar patterns and findings.

ARCHIVAL USE-OF-FORCE DATA

The policy change that is the subject of this study was made in an attempt to decrease the use of tasers in low-intensity encounters by increasing the level of resistance that must be present to authorize deployment. Essentially, the change raised the level of resistance from passive resistance to active resistance. This means that suspects must be actively resisting the actions of the officer—by pulling away or fleeing, not just passively resisting—for a taser to be deployed. For the purposes of this examination, data was captured both before and after the policy change.

During both of the identified time periods for analysis 890 use-of-force incidents with a taser were recorded by Orlando police officers. This data was separated into two samples, labeled Pretest and Posttest. In the period between June 4, 2003 and June 3, 2004, one year prior to the policy change (Pretest), officers recorded 523 taser uses. In the period between June 5, 2004 and June 5, 2005, one year after the policy change (Posttest), officers recorded 367 taser uses. Descriptive statistics for situational level characteristics of the suspects are presented in Table 12 below.

---

[3] The terms resistance and response continuum are unique to the OPD when referring to their Use-of-Force Continuum. This terminology is used interchangeably throughout this study.

Table 12: Situational Level Variables—OPD Use-of-Force Report Data—Pretest/Posttest

Variable/Value	Total Sample		Pretest		Posttest		Test Statistic	Sig. Value
	N	Pct	N	Pct	N	Pct		
Suspect Race								
Black	461	51.8	273	52.2	188	51.2	x^2=5.178	.270
White	315	35.4	189	36.1	126	34.3		
Hispanic	111	12.5	61	11.7	50	13.6		
Asian	2	.2	0	0	2	.5		
Other	1	.1	0	0	1	.3		
Total	890	100.0	523	100.0	367	100.0		
Suspect Gender								
Male	820	92.1	474	90.6	346	94.3	x^2=3.958	.047*
Female	70	7.9	49	9.4	21	5.7		
Total	890	100.0	523	100.0	367	100.0		
Suspect Age								
Under 12	3	.3	3	0.6	0	0	T=.164	.870
13-17	50	5.6	26	5.1	24	6.5		
18-20	88	9.9	61	12.0	27	7.5		
21-29	383	43.0	211	41.4	172	47.3		
30-44	278	31.2	168	32.9	110	30.0		
45-59	60	6.7	38	7.5	22	5.4		
60+	6	.7	3	0.6	3	0.8		
Unknown	22	2.5	13	2.5	10	2.6		
Total	890	100.0	523	100.0	367	100.0		

The descriptive statistics on the individual-level suspect variables were unremarkable. As expected, the majority of suspects encountered in use-of-force encounters were males (92.1%). Unformed Crime Report data and prior research have found that males are involved in 80 % of all violent encounters (Riksheim and Chermak, 1993; Garner et al. 1995, 1996; Terrill and Mastrofski, 2002).

An examination of the suspect race and age data revealed that a majority of suspects (51%) were Black, (35%) were White, (12%) of the suspects were Hispanic and (.3 %) were Asian or Other. The majority of suspects (43%) were between 21-29 years of age. Only (5%) of the suspects were juveniles.

As shown in Table 12, there does not appear to be an appreciable difference in the situational-level variables related to the suspects between the two reporting periods. Both the age (T=.164, *df*=866, *p*=.870) and race (chi square value=5.178, *df*=4, *p*=.270) of these individuals appeared to be relatively the same. However, tasers appear to have been used less against females in the period after the policy change than before. This difference is statistically significant (chi square value=3.958, *df*=1, *p*=.047). It is probable that since females are not as likely to engage officers in hand-to-hand fighting, officers may have been less prone to use these electronic devices in use-of-force scenarios, especially after this shift in policy.

For comparison purposes, key situational variable data relevant to the police-citizen encounters are presented in Table 13. These data are stratified by the period in which they occurred. The table illustrates these subdivisions and tests to see if there is a significant difference between the two periods based on these situational variables, using either chi-square or t-tests. Chi square tests were run on the variables suspect injured, officer injured, and officer self-initiated variables. Chi square tests were used to determine if the nominal variables in the study models are related. Independent sample t-tests were used to conduct means testing. A t-test was run on number of officers, suspects and citizens present, severity of suspect injury, level of suspect resistance and threat level as these were treated as interval-level variables.

Individual-level variable data on the officers involved in police-citizen encounters are also presented in Table 13. Chi square tests were run on the variables officer gender and officer race. T-tests were run on the variables officer tenure and officer age.

According to the extant literature, one of the prime determinants of the nature of police- citizen encounters involves situational-level elements. In fact, Freidrich (1980) separated his analysis into three different levels (individual, situational, and organizational) and found that situational-level variables are oftentimes the most important. These situational variables include data on the suspect (race, gender, age or size) and data on the type of encounter (self-initiated, felony crime in progress, or traffic stop). Individual level variables typically involve data related to the officer (tenure, levels of education) or officer demographics. Hence, it is prudent to examine these situational-level variables across both time periods to see if there is a difference between them. If there is a difference, it could indicate that tasers are being used almost exclusively in very dangerous situations. However, if there is no difference, it could be an indicator that these contextual variables play little role in an officer's decision to use this less-than-lethal weapon.

In this regard, it is prudent to examine the number of officers present at a given encounter. A high number of officers tends to indicate a tense situation where there is likely to be a possibility of injury to either the officer or a suspect. However, when we examine the data, there does not appear to be any difference in the number of officers present at these use-of-force encounters. T-tests were run to confirm this and failed to reach the required level to claim that there were appreciable differences regarding this variable (T = -.255, df=888, p=.822).

Table 13: Situational Level Variables—OPD Use-of-Force Report Data—Pretest/Posttest

Variable/Value Label	Total Sample		Pretest		Posttest		Test	Sig.
	N	Pct	N	Pct	N	Pct	Statistic	Value
Threat or Seriousness of Encounter								
Low Threat	274	30.8	170	32.5	104	28.3		
Medium Threat	458	51.5	267	51.1	191	52.0	T=-1.576	.115
High Threat	158	17.8	86	16.4	72	19.6		
Total	890	100.0	523	100.0	367	100.0		
Number of Citizen Bystanders								
0	563	63.4	342	65.4	221	60.2		
1	156	17.7	91	17.4	65	17.7		
2	89	9.8	49	9.4	40	10.9		
3	46	5.2	23	4.4	23	6.3	T=-1.820	.069
4	24	2.5	10	1.9	14	3.8		
More than 4	4	1.3	8	1.5	4	1.1		
Total	890	100.0	5235	100.0	367	100.0		
Officer Self Initiated								
yes	473	53.1	276	52.8	197	53.7	x^2=.071	.790
no	417	46.9	247	47.2	170	46.3		
Total	890	100.0	523	100.0	367	100.0		
Officer Gender								
Male	841	94.4	503	96.1	338	92.0	x^2=6.893	.009*
Female	49	5.6	20	3.9	29	8.0		
Total	890	100.0	523	100.0	367	100.0		

Table 13, cont.

Variable/Value Label	Total Sample N	Pct	Pretest N	Pct	Posttest N	Pct	Test Statistic	Sig. Value
Officer Race								
Black	158	17.8	80	15.3	78	21.2		
White	625	70.3	378	72.3	247	67.4	x^2=15.868	.003*
Hispanic	71	7.9	41	7.9	30	8.2		
Asian	29	3.3	23	4.4	6	1.6		
Other	7	.7	1	.1	6	1.6		
Total	890	100.0	523	100.0	367	100.0		
Officer Tenure	N	Pct						
1-5	54	16.3						
6-10	146	43.8						
11-15	58	17.4					T=.700	.484
16-20	61	18.3						
21-30	13	3.9						
30+	1	.3						
Total Sample	333	100.0						
Officer Age								
21-25	2	.6						
26-30	27	8.1						
31-40	167	50.1					T=.951	.342
41-50	117	35.1						
51-60	19	5.7						
61+	0	0						
Total	333	100.0						

Data on the number of suspects present during an encounter was also examined. This is also an important factor as the number of suspects present might be a significant influence on the level of force used. Again, t-tests were run to confirm this and failed to reach the required level to claim that there were appreciable differences related to this variable (T = -1.093, *df*=887.992, *p*=.275).

As far as injuries to officers were concerned, these data indicate that officers were not injured any more frequently in the posttest period. A chi square test was run, and it was determined that there was no higher probability of officers being injured in the posttest period (chi square value =3.059, *df* =1, *p*=.080). This finding does not reach the level of statistical significance at the .05 level. Given the small sample size (N=890), a larger sample of archival data might produce a different result. Further research with a larger sample is needed to more thoroughly investigate this research question.

Data on the frequency of suspect injury were also examined. The data indicate that the difference in the percentages of suspect injury was not statistically significant. In fact, when a chi square test was run, there was no difference in the likelihood of a suspect being injured either before or after the change in policy (chi square value =.337, *df* =1, *p*=.562). This is likely because all of those who are in the sample suffered the same type of injury from the penetration of the taser darts.

Additional data were collected on the nature and severity of the injuries suffered by the suspects. Treating this variable as an interval-level measure since there was some ordering to the data, a t-test was run and it confirmed that there was no statistical difference in the severity of the injuries suffered in either period (T=-.929, *df*=721.935, *p*=.353).

Also examined were data on suspect resistance. The pattern clearly shows that suspects tended to resist at higher levels in the posttest period, which was consistent with the organizational change in policy that raised the authorized level on the Use-of-Force Continuum when tasers can be used. Based on t-test results, the difference is statistically significant at the .05 level

(T =-4.847, *df* =749.620, *p* =.000). An examination of data on the level of suspect resistance reveals that in 8 uses of force incidents in the posttest group (after the change in policy) the suspects were resisting at a passive level of resistance when a taser was deployed. Anecdotally, this would seem to indicate that the use of tasers in these low intensity incidents violated the agency policy. The incident data reveals that 7 of the 8 events occurred within four weeks of the policy change between June 5, 2004 and July 6, 2004. This may indicate that some officers had not yet adjusted to the policy change or that a training issue could be to blame. There was no distinct pattern or other common variables in these events. Each of these incidents involved different officers. The types of incidents that led to these uses of force were from a variety of low, medium and high threat level encounters. Half of these incidents involved officer self initiated action and the other were dispatched. These incidents only comprise 2.2% of the total posttest data.

The effect of threat level or seriousness of the encounter was also examined. The level of threat encountered by officers was not found to be statistically significant, which was confirmed by t-tests (T =-1.576, *df*=888, *p*=.115). It was not expected that the threat levels would change between the pretest and posttest groups. The data examined relating to police activity remained very constant between the three threat level categories, with the majority falling into the low or medium threat-level categories in both the pre and posttest groups.

Data on the presence of citizen bystanders were also examined. Using a one-tailed solution, a significant difference in presence or number of citizen bystanders was found. In this case, there were more citizens present in the typical posttest use of force incident than in the pretest, indicating the situations where tasers were used were more likely more serious and had a higher probably of escalating to a more violent and volatile encounter. This was determined by a t-test (T =-1.820, *df*=745.311, *p*=.069). A one-tailed solution was used because prior research has identified the presence of citizens as having an effect on the levels of police force; this was not a significant factor in this data set. This finding could also be explained by the increased public awareness of the controversy surrounding taser use by police. It is possible that taser usage by police may have aroused more public curiosity after the media attention regarding its use. This would account for the presence of more citizen bystanders in the posttest group.

The influence of officer self-initiated contacts versus dispatched calls for service :was also examined using a chi square test (chi square value = .071, df =1, p= .790). An analysis of this data indicates that there was no statistically significant difference in the levels of officer self-initiated or dispatched calls for service in either the pretest or the posttest groups.

These preliminary analyses show that, for the most part, there are very few differences in the situational characteristics (suspect race, gender, and age) or the characteristics related to the incident (number of officers present, number of suspects present, officers injured, suspects injured, suspect injury type, suspect level of resistance, threat level of the encounter, number of citizen bystanders present, and whether or not the encounter was officer-initiated or a call for service) :in the encounters between the pretest and posttest. The only major differences between these variables appeared to be with suspects; namely, officers generally used taser less against females.

Various research studies have examined the influence of officer demographics on police-citizen encounters (Garner et al. 1995, 1996; Terrill, 2001, 2003). The influence of individual level variables related to officers involved in use of force encounters were also examined in this study. Officer age, gender, race and agency tenure were all examined to determine if the influence of these variables was statistically significant. There does not appear to be a measurable difference in the individual-level variables related to the officers' age and experience between the pretest and posttest periods. Both the age (T=.951, df=888, p=.342) and tenure (T=.700, df=888, p=.484) of the officers appeared to be relatively the same in the both groups. It does appears that female officers used force 4.9% more often in the posttest group (chi square=6.893, df=1, p=.009). Also found to be significant was the influence of officer race in use of force encounters between the pretest and posttest groups (chi square=15.868, *df*=4, *p*=.003). An examination of the data on officer race reveals that while white officers used force 4.9 % less often in the posttest period, black officers used force 5.9% more often. This is an interesting finding that warrants further examination and study. Use of force incidents by Hispanic, Asian, and other officers did not significantly change. As far as the situational-level variables related to event itself, officers appeared to use tasers, on average, more against suspects that were offering more aggressive resistance, and where there was a crowd assembled.

The following research questions are related to the examination of the archival use-of-force data. By having some background knowledge of the sample data on use of force, this allows us to move forward and begin testing the research questions of interest.

RESEARCH QUESTIONS FROM ARCHIVAL USE-OF-FORCE DATA

One of the principal concerns of taser use and one of the reasons why it generates public interest is the issue of how often and when tasers are used in use-of-force incidents. The policy changes that were implemented by the OPD were specifically designed to reduce taser use by imposing more stringent restrictions as to when officers' can use tasers. This makes examining what effect the policy change has had on the frequency of taser use a significant area of study.

Research Question 1: Frequency of Taser Deployments

Research Question 1, related to the frequency of taser deployments, posited that raising the authorized level on the Use-of-Force Continuum for taser deployment has decreased the frequency of taser deployments. The related null hypothesis posed that raising the authorized level for taser use on the Use-of-Force Continuum has had no effect on the frequency of taser use by officers. The hypotheses for this research question are given below.

   HO_1: Raising the authorized level for taser use on the Use-of-Force Continuum has had no effect on the frequency of taser use by officers.

   $H1_1$: Raising the authorized level for taser use on the Use-of-Force Continuum has decreased the frequency of taser use by officers.

To address this question, one can simply count the number of deployments and see if the raw frequency has increased. However, that would not provide the reader with an adequate picture of the probability of true deployments because most use-of-force incidents usually coincide with an arrest. If there were more arrests in the pretest period, then the raw frequency would be inflated. Thus, the only way to get an adequate picture and/or understanding of this is to use a test that measures differences of proportions.

To address this research question, OPD call-for-service, arrest, and total uses of force data during the pre and posttest periods was examined. During the pretest period, from June 2003 through June 2004, OPD officers handled 337,470 calls for service, made 19,267 arrests, and used all types of authorized force in 707 incidents. This includes the use of OC spray, ASP baton, and weaponless tactics such as strikes and takedowns. During the posttest period, from June 2004 through June 2005, OPD officers handled 383,567 calls for service, made 19,770 arrests and used force in 572 encounters. The use of ::arrestcall-for-service, arrest, and use of force data to address the question of the effect on frequency of taser resulting from the organizational change is warranted based on the fluctuation in the crime rate and accompanying police activity used to counter it during the analysis periods. An examination of Uniformed Crime Report data for Orlando during the periods of analysis reveals a 3% reduction in the index crime rate per 100,000 populations between 2003 and 2004. It is important to note that only the six months of June through December 2003 are included in the analysis period. The change in index crime rate between

2004 and 2005 was recorded as a 3.5% increase (FDLE, 2003, 2004, 2005). The analysis period ended in June 2005. These data are three such measures of that activity and are used to demonstrate the overall increase in police activity during the study periods and then to incorporate taser deployment data to test hypotheses on the effect of the organizational change relating to when the taser could be used.

During the pretest period 523 taser deployments were recorded in use-of-force encounters by officers. The numbers of taser deployments during the posttest period were 367, indicating that the number of deployments dropped by 156 actual uses or 29 %. The total numbers of use of force by officers also decreased by 135 incidents, or 19%, from 707 to 572 in the pretest and posttest periods. To analyze these data the proper way, a Z test for the difference in proportions was applied to the arrests, calls for service, and total use of force encounter data in the pretest and posttest samples. The results are illustrated in Table 14.

Table 14: Z Test for Difference in Proportions in Taser Deployments in the Pre and Posttest Periods Using Number of Arrests, Calls for Service, and Use of Force Data

	Arrests	Calls for Service	Total Use of Force Encounters
Z-Values	5.68	7.15	3.83
Critical Values	(1.65)	(1.65)	(1.65)

The Z test for the differences in two proportions is designed to determine whether there is a difference between two population proportions and whether one is larger than the other, which is a one-tailed test. To use this test, certain assumptions must be met. These are: (1) independent samples, (2) a normal binomial distribution, and (3) a large enough sample size ($np \geq 5$ and $n[1-p] \geq 5$ for each population). For purposes of this analysis, all of these assumptions have been met.

The following formula was used to compute the Z test:

$$Z = \frac{(ps_1 - ps_2) - (p_1 - p_2)}{\sqrt{|p|(1-|p|)}\left(\dfrac{1}{n_1} + \dfrac{1}{n_2}\right)}$$

Figure 2: Calculation of the Test Statistic

After computing the Z test using arrest data, the Z value was 5.68, and the critical value was 1.65. Therefore, since the Z value was higher than its critical value, this result supports that there is a difference in proportion between the ratio of taser uses/arrests between the pre and posttest samples. After computing the Z test using call-for-service data, the Z value was 7.15, and the critical value of Z was 1.65. Since the Z value was higher than its critical value, we can also claim that there is a difference in proportion between the ratio of taser uses/call for service between the pre and posttest samples. Using the same Z test analysis with total use of force data, the Z value was 3.83, and the critical value of Z was 1.65. Since the Z value was higher than its critical value, we can also claim that there is a difference in proportion between the ratio of taser uses/total use of forces between the pre and posttest samples.

Using arrest, calls-for-service, and use of force data for analysis, the findings are that tasers were used more frequently in the pretest sample. This finding substantiates a reduction of taser use in the posttest sample. A reduction in overall use of force incidents was also found. Based on this finding, we can reject the null hypothesis and state that the change in organizational policy related to taser placement on the Use-of-Force Continuum may have had a significant effect on the frequency of taser use. That change is a measurable reduction in the frequency of taser use after the change in organizational policy.

The level of resistance offered by suspects in a use-of-force encounter is one of the fundamental questions of this study. The policy change examined specifically raises the required level of resistance that must be present for the taser to be used. The effect on levels of suspect resistance after the policy change is the focus of the research question addressed below.

Research Question 2: Level of Suspect Resistance

Research Question 2 posed if raising the authorized level on the Use-of-Force Continuum for taser deployment would result in deployments that are more serious when the suspect actively resists the officer to a greater degree. The null hypothesis related to this question states that there is no difference in the levels of suspect resistance encountered by officers after the change in organizational policy. For this research question, the research and null hypotheses are:

$H0_2$: There is no difference in the levels of suspect resistance encountered by officers after the change in organizational police.

$H1_2$: There will be a difference in levels of suspect resistance encountered by officers after the change in organizational police.

An independent samples *t*-test and regression analysis was completed to test this hypothesis. An independent samples *t*-test is used to compare the mean scores of two different groups of people or conditions to determine if there is a significant difference between the groups (Norušis, 2005).

Group statistics for pre and posttest results from the variable suspect resistance are given in Table 15. These results indicate that the mean result for the pretest group was 2.04, with a Standard Deviation (SD) of .434. The mean for the posttest group was 2.19, with a SD of .468. The results for the independent samples *t*-test were significant at the .000 level, suggesting that there was indeed a difference between the levels of resistance offered by suspects between the two reporting periods.

Table 15: Group Statistics for Suspect Level of Resistance

Test Period	N	Mean	SD	T-Value	Sig.
Pretest	523	2.04	.434		
Posttest	367	2.19	.468	-4.784	.000

While it is easy to say that the means or distributions are different, it is difficult to state that this one specific finding provides direct support to the hypothesis that the change in policy was the sole reason why suspects resisted less. However, what would provide more support is if the inclusion of additional correlates does not diminish the differences found here. Hence, a multiple regression equation was run to check and make sure that higher levels of resistance are not caused by some other factor. The use of a multiple regression test extends the bivariate analysis. This also allows for identifying when a change in nature or direction of the relationship occurs when the effects of significant variables are controlled. Typically, the use of OLS regression with ordinal level dependent variables would not be the preferred method of analysis. However, in this case OLS was used in lieu of Ordered Logit or Ordered Probit Regression to make the interpretation of analysis results easier for the reader. This is supported by Sturman (1996) who found that despite methodological expectations the use of OLS regression does not produce significantly more false positives than expected. While an ordered probit model appears to be a viable solution, it is not without problems. Aldrich and Nelson (1985) and Menard (1995) claim that ordered probit estimates often produce predicted values of the dependent variable that lie out of the range of the dependent variable. This happens for three reasons. First, the formula under the proportional odds assumption assumes that changes in the dependent variable will be stochastic across all cross-category comparisons within the dependent variable. That is, the effect coefficient (and thus error terms) produced and simultaneously estimated during the program's maximum likelihood iterations must be invariant across categories both higher and lower to the predicted value. If heteroskedasticity is apparent within an estimated model, errant values are likely. The second cause of problems using models with a limited range dependent variable model is that a series of extremely large or small values in one of the explanatory variables may distort the distribution and variability of the residuals, which in turn will influence the model's predictive power (Aldrich and Nelson 1984; Schroeder et al. 1986). Third, Greene (1992) states that since the both the ordered probit and logit models depend heavily on the cross-classification algorithm, the presence of non-empty cells may cause the estimation process to either breakdown or produce faulty estimates. Thus, ordered probit does not allow of stable and easy interpretation of the effect of explanatory variables on a limited range dependent variable even if it does represent an underlying latent scale. This problem is further exacerbated when the number of categories of the dependent variable exceeds three and the number of independent or covariates exceed one. In these cases, it may be better to use multiple regression, noting that the effect estimate of the independent variable is a conservative estimate, although significant in the appropriate direction (Kennedy, 1992; Menard, 1995). Bohnstedt and Carter (1971) and Busemeyer and Jones (1983) claim that ignoring the true properties of ordinal level data and treating them an interval using some inferential methods rarely effect the making of a Type I or Type II error.

The model summary presents an R Square value of .075, which indicates that this model is 7.5% better at estimating the value of the dependent variable by knowing the values of the independent variables. The F-test confirms this assertion.

The multiple regression equation in Table 16 tests this hypothesis. In this model, we include the variable representing the type of test as well as a series of other situational-level and individual officer-level correlates of police force. Overall, the model is robust and represents a significant increase in the explanatory power by the value of F (5.478) and its corresponding significance value (.000). The results of the model suggest that, controlling for other factors present, on average there were higher levels of resistance in the posttest period. Further, other factors may contribute to the increased level of suspect resistance. These factors include the number of officers and suspects present as well as the seriousness of injury inflicted upon the suspect. For each of these variables, the relationship is positive. Thus, the more officers and suspects present at an encounter, or the more likely an individual is to receive serious injuries, the more likely we are to see increased levels of force. None of the situational-level variables related to officer characteristics were found to be significant indicators of suspect resistance.

Table 16: Level of Suspect Resistance— Ordinary Least Squares Regression

	b	SE *b*	Beta	*t*	*p*
Constant	1.842	.165		11.159	.000
Pretest or Posttest	.141	.030	.153	4.637	.000
Situational Characteristics					
No. Primary Officers	.054	.022	.081	2.430	.015
No. Suspects	.142	.073	.065	1.948	.052
Citizen bystanders	.014	.013	.036	1.068	.286
Threat or Seriousness of encounter	.030	.022	.046	1.374	.170
Suspect Injury Type	.066	.017	.128	3.771	.000
Suspect Sex	-.059	.055	-.035	-1.071	.285
Suspect Black	-.060	.033	-.066	-1.781	.075
Suspect Hispanic	.002	.049	.002	.049	.961
Officer Characteristics					
Officer Age	-.003	.003	-.039	-.894	.372
Officer Gender	-.037	.066	-.019	-.562	.574
Officer Tenure	.000	.004	.003	.066	.948
Officer Race	.004	.022	.007	.197	.844

R^2=.075
df = 13
F =5.478
F significance<.000

The analysis findings indicate that a statistically significant difference in the level of suspect resistance was present after the change in agency policy. The levels of suspect resistance increased after the change in policy related to taser deployment. Based on this finding, the null hypothesis is rejected, and a significant difference in the levels of suspect resistance encountered by officers was observed after the change in organizational policy.

Another fundamental question of this study is what effect the policy change had on the frequency of injuries to suspects. The safety of suspects in use-of-force encounters is a significant issue for public safety organizations. The following question specifically examines what effect raising the authorized level of resistance required for taser use had on the frequency of injuries to suspects in use-of-force encounters.

Research Question 3: Frequency of Injuries to Suspects

Research question 3 posited if raising the authorized level on the Use-of-Force Continuum for taser deployment has resulted in a change in the number of injuries suffered by suspects in police-citizen encounters. The null hypothesis related to this question states that raising the authorized level on the Use-of-Force Continuum for taser deployment has resulted in no change in the number of injuries suffered by suspects in police-citizen encounters. The hypotheses for this research question are:

$H0_3$: There is no difference in the number of suspect injuries after the change in organizational policy

$H1_3$: There is a difference in the number of suspect injuries after the change in organizational policy

The results of a cross-tabulation of the data on Suspect Injuries in the pretest and posttest groups are depicted in Table 17. To address this research question, a Pearson's Chi square test for independence was conducted using the Suspect injured nominal variable. The Pearson's Chi square test is a nonparametric statistical test that mathematically seeks to determine if two or more variables are distributed equally. This statistic is used to test the hypothesis of no association of the identified variable data. The Chi square test results also are depicted in Table 17.

**Table 17: Chi Square Test for the Frequency of Injury
to Suspects**

Suspect Injured		No	Yes	Total	df	x^2	Sig.
	Pretest	139	384	523	1	.337	.562
	Posttest	104	263	367			
		243	647	890			

Based on the results depicted in Table 17, the Pearson Chi square value of .337 does not meet the required level to be considered significant at the .05 level. Based on this result, the null hypothesis is not rejected. This finding supports that there is no difference in the overall number of suspects injured between the two reporting periods. Thus, it appears that the change in the organizational policy concerning when tasers should be deployed has likely had no impact on the number of suspects injured.

The change in severity of injuries to suspects resulting from the policy change is another important area for examination. How severely suspects are injured in use-of-force encounters is one of the primary concerns of both the police and the public. One of the purposes of the Use-of-Force Continuum and the policies that guide its use are the reduction of injuries to police officers and suspects. The effect on severity of injuries to suspects after the policy change is the focus of the following research question.

Research Question 4: Severity of Injuries to Suspects

Research Question 4 addressed the issue of whether raising the authorized level of force for using tasers has had any effect on the severity of injuries to suspects. This question is different from the previous one in that it is not just asking if the raw number of injuries changed after the change in policy, but, rather, it is looking to see if the severity of these injuries changed. Since tasers would only be used in higher risk police-citizen encounters after the change in policy, it is likely that the severity of these injuries would have, on average, increased. The research and null hypotheses for this research question are:

HO_4: There is no difference in the severity of suspect injuries suffered by citizens in police-citizen encounters after the change in organizational policy

$H1_4$: There is a difference in the severity of suspect injuries suffered by citizens in police-citizen encounters after the change in organizational policy

Group statistics for pre and posttest results for the Suspect injury type variable are presented in Table 18. These results indicate that, for the pretest group, the mean was 2.02, with a standard deviation of .835. The mean for the posttest group was 2.08, with a standard deviation of .949. An independent samples *t*-test and regression model were performed to test this hypothesis.

Table 18: Group Statistics for Severity of Suspect Injury

Test Period	N	Mean	SD	T-Value	Sig.
Pretest	523	2.02	.835		
Posttest	367	2.08	.949	-.929	.353

As shown in Table 18, the results for the independent *t*-test indicate that there is no difference in the level of suspect injury between the two reporting periods. Based on this finding the null hypothesis is not rejected. This supports that, on average, the level or severity of suspect injury between the reporting periods is roughly the same. No violations of normality were noted between groups.

Since the *t*-test does not allow for examination of other control variables and how the addition of these other variants may influence the test, a multiple regression model was run to take these other factors into account. The use of a multiple regression model extends the bivariate analysis. This allows for identifying when a change in nature or direction of the relationship occurs when significant variables in the model are controlled.

Table 19 presents the results of the regression model using suspect injury type as the dependent variable and using pretest and posttest, number of primary officers, number of suspects, the number of citizen bystanders, threat or seriousness of encounter, suspect resistance, suspect sex, suspect black, suspect hispanic, officer age, officer gender, officer tenure and officer race as the independent variables.

Table 19: Suspect Injury Type— Ordinary Least Squares Regression

	b	SE *b*	Beta	*t*	*p*
Constant	.893	.339		2.638	.008
Pretest or Posttest	.011	.059	.006	.192	.848
Situational Characteristics					
No. primary officers	.123	.043	.095	2.870	.004
No. suspects	.114	.140	.027	.812	.460
Citizen bystanders	.098	.026	.127	3.825	.000
Threat or seriousness of encounter	-.062	.042	-.048	-1.459	.145
Suspect resistance	.243	.065	.125	3.771	.000
Suspect Sex	.230	.107	.070	2.157	.031
Suspect Black	-.281	.064	-.159	-4.403	.000
Suspect Hispanic	-.003	.094	-.001	-.032	.974
Officer Characteristics					
Officer Age	.004	.007	.028	.655	.513
Officer Gender	.265	.126	.068	2.098	.036
Officer Tenure	-.011	.008	-.058	-1.336	.182
Officer Race	.007	.043	.005	.165	.869

R^2= .096
df= 13
F= 7.174
F significance<.008

The model summary presents an R Square value of .096, which indicates that this model explains 9.6% of the total variance of the dependent variable. The F-test confirms this assertion. Overall, the model is robust and represents a significant increase in the explanatory power by the value of F (7.174) and its corresponding significance value (.008). When examining the regression results, the significant predictors of the severity of suspect injury include the number of officers and citizens at a scene, the level of suspect resistance, if the suspect was male, and if the suspect was not of African American descent. The presence of more officers and bystanders at a scene are likely to increase the severity of injury. Further, the more the suspect resists, the more likely they are to be injured. The only predictor of severity of injury related to officer characteristics was officer gender. An examination of the breakdown of officer demographics in both the pretest and posttest data reveals that female officers used force 4.9% more often in the posttest group. Of critical importance in this model is that the levels of suspect resistance (pretest vs. posttest) failed to reach the required level of statistical significance, thus confirming the bivariate relationship tested by the earlier *t*-test.

One of the serendipitous findings in this model is related to the race of the suspect. Suspects of African-American heritage experienced less serious injuries than those of other races. This finding is difficult to interpret; however, what it appears to say is that it is possible that this class may resist less and, thus, be less likely to be injured more seriously. This argument is supported by the previous regression in that African-Americans were significantly less likely to resist at higher levels when a two-tailed solution was employed (See Table 16). It may be that this class of citizens have had tasers used against them in the past and, thus, appear to have more experience with the efficiency of these weapons. This, however, is only conjecture and should be tested by further research.

Research Question 5: Frequency of Injuries to Officers

Research question 5 posited a similar question. However, this question asked if raising the level of force on the Use-of-Force Continuum changed the frequency of injury to officers. This question is important because we would expect that after the change in policy regarding where the use of tasers are viewed as appropriate, we would expect that the number of injuries to officers would increase since the organization is limiting the available options for dealing with potentially dangerous suspects. For this research question, the research and null hypotheses are:

HO_5: There is no difference in the number of officer injuries after the change in organizational policy.

$H1_5$: There is a difference in the number of officer injuries after the change in organizational policy.

To address this research question, a chi square test of independence was conducted using the nominal variable officer injured and the reporting period was run. The results of the cross-tabulation are provided in Table 15. The data in this table reveal that officers were injured in only 4.6 percent of the cases in the first reporting period. After the change in policy, however, officers were injured in 7.4 percent of these encounters. While it does appear that officers were injured more after the change in policy, this difference of 2.8 percent may not be different from 0 in a statistical sense. Hence, a chi-square test was run to test to see if this difference was large enough to claim that there was a statistical difference in these two reporting periods. Table 20 provides the chi square test results.

Table 20: Chi Square Test for the Frequency of Injury to Officers

Officer Injured	No	Yes	Total	df	x^2	Sig.
Pretest	499	24	523	1	3.059	.080
Posttest	340	27	367			
	839	51	890			

Based on the results shown in Table 20, the Pearson chi square value of 3.059 is not significant at the .05 level. As previously stated, while this finding does not reach the level of statistical significance at the .05 level, a larger sample of archival data might produce a different result. Further research is warranted to more thoroughly explore this research question.

Based on this finding the null hypothesis is not rejected. This supports that there does not appear to be a difference in the number of officer injuries between the two reporting periods.

The frequency of injuries to officers did not significantly change as organizational policy limited the use of tasers to only those encounters involving higher levels of force.

OFFICER SURVEY RESPONSE DATA

To capture data related to officers' perceptions of the effect of organizational policy change and taser use, a survey instrument was administered to a purposeful sample of 333 OPD officers. The officers chosen to participate in the survey were identified by examining the archival use-of-force data and selecting officers who deployed tasers during both the pre and posttest periods. Only those officers who deployed a taser during these time periods and who were still employed by the OPD were chosen to participate in the survey. From the total number of officers contacted 130 completed surveys were returned, resulting in a response rate of 39 percent. (See Table 6 for a comparison of survey sample population and OPD population demographics).

The survey instrument consisted of questions designed to capture officers' perceptions of how the change in organizational policy relating to taser placement on the Use-of-Force Continuum has affected their safety and the safety of suspects in use-of-force encounters. The survey also captured demographic information on the officers' educational level, job assignments during the archival data study period, rank, agency tenure, and previous employment in law enforcement.

A series of survey questions were posed to officers in a variety of subject areas related to the effect of the policy change on taser use and taser effectiveness. These questions asked how the policy change effected: the risk of injury to suspects, the risk of injury to officers, the proper placement of the taser on the Use-of-Force Continuum, and the effectiveness of the taser in subduing noncompliant or combative suspects. Table 21 provides the respondents' demographic data.

Table 21: Respondent Demographic Data from Survey Instrument

Variable	Value	N	Pct
Officer Race	Black	11	8.5
	White	99	76.2
	Hispanic	14	10.8
	Asian	4	3.1
	Other	1	.8
	Missing	1	.8
	Total	130	100.0
Officer Gender	Male	119	91.5
	Female	11	8.5
	Total	130	100.0
Rank in PD between 6/03 – 7/05	Police Officer	111	85.4
	Master Police Officer	3	2.3
	Detective	12	9.2
	Sergeant	3	2.3
	Lieutenant	0	0.0
	Skipped question	1	.8
	Total	130	100.0
Officer Age	N	127	
	Minimum age	25	
	Maximum age	54	
	Mean	37.5	
	SD	6.264	
Worked for another L.E. agency?	No	58	44.6
	Yes	72	55.4
	Total	130	100.0
Officer level of education	Less than high school diploma	0.0	0.0
	High School Diploma or GED	7	5.4
	Some junior college but did not earn a degree	20	15.4
	Associates Degree	16	12.3
	More than two years of college but did not earn a degree	9	6.9

Table 21, cont.

Variable	Value	N	Pct
	Bachelors degree	53	40.8
	Some graduate courses but did not earn a graduate degree	15	11.5
	Graduate degree	9	6.9
	Skipped question	1	.8
	Total	130	100.0
Assignment in PD between 6/03 – 7/05	Patrol	109	83.8
	Tactical	4	3.1
	Detectives	12	9.2
	Narcotics	3	2.3
	Motors	1	.8
	Skipped question	1	.8
	Total	130	100.0
Law enforcement officer tenure	N	130	
	Minimum Years	3	
	Maximum Years	33	
	Mean	11.4	
	SD	6.16	
Orlando Police Department tenure	N	130	
	Minimum Years	3	
	Maximum Years	33	
	Mean	9.45	
	SD	5.2	

RESEARCH QUESTIONS FROM OFFICER SURVEY RESPONSE DATA

It is important to examine officer perceptions related to the key elements of this study to compare how officers perceive the change has effected their safety, the safety of suspects, and the effectiveness of the taser as a use-of-force method. Officer perceptions relating to these areas are compared to the findings in the archival use-of-force data. By making this comparison, the goal is for a better understanding of the aggregate effect of the policy changes on taser use and effectiveness. Research question 6 asks officers their perception on whether or not the change in organizational policy has increased the risk of harm to officers. The purpose of this analysis is to see if officer perceptions match with the behavior depicted in the archival data from police use-of-force encounters. The analysis of archival data revealed that the frequency of taser use by officers decreased, while the levels of suspect resistance encountered by officers after the policy change increased. There was no change in the frequency or severity of injuries to suspects as result of the policy change. There was also no statistically significant increase in the frequency of injuries to officers after the policy change. A comparison of the results of the archival data analysis and the officers' perceptions will generate valuable findings for discussion and further investigation.

Research Question 6: Officers' Perception of Increased Risk of Harm to Themselves as a Result of Organizational Policy Change

Research question 6 asked if officers perceive that the change in organizational policy on the authorized level on the Use-of-Force Continuum for when the taser can be used has increased the risk of harm to them in a use-of-force encounter. It is important to examine officer perceptions related to the change in risk to them resulting from the policy change as this may have an effect on how frequently they deploy the taser and their level of confidence with it as a use-of-force method. If officers feel constrained by the more stringent guidelines of the policy change, they may opt not to deploy tasers and use some other method of control. It is also important to compare the archival data on the frequency of injury to officers to see if it matches with the archival data from use-of-force encounters.

   HO_6: Officers express no preference regarding whether the change in organizational policy relating to when the taser can be used increases the risk of harm to them in a use-of-force encounter.

H1$_6$: Officers perceive that the change in organizational policy relating to when the taser can be used increases the risk of harm to them in a use-of-force encounter.

Four questions on the survey instrument were asked to capture officers' perceptions relating to the increased risk to them from the change in agency policy. Officers were first asked their level of agreement to the statement that: "The policy change relating to placement of the taser (ECD) on the resistance and response continuum increases the risk of harm to you from suspects during a use-of-force incident." Table 22 provides the results for this question.

Table 22: Officer's Opinions on Change in Policy Increasing the Potential Harm to Officers

Level of Agreement	N	Percentage
Strongly Disagree	16	12.3
Disagree	33	25.4
Neutral	4	3.1
Agreed	53	40.8
Strongly Agreed	24	18.5
Total	130	100.1

* Percentages may not equal 100% due to rounding error

As shown in Table 22, the majority of the respondents, 59.3% (77), agreed or strongly agreed with this survey question. This would indicate that a majority of the respondents perceived that the organizational change that raised the level of resistance on the Use-of-Force Continuum where taser use is authorized increased their risk of harm during a use-of-force encounter.

A second question on the survey instrument asked officers their level of agreement to the statement "Based on your experience would you say that being equipped with a taser makes you safer when working as a police officer." Table 23 provides the results for this question.

Table 23: Officers Opinions on Possession of Taser and Officer Safety

Level of Agreement	N	Percentage
Strongly Disagree	5	3.8
Disagree	7	5.4
Neutral	8	6.2
Agreed	38	29.2
Strongly Agreed	72	55.4
Total	130	100.0

* Percentages may not equal 100% due to rounding error

As in the previous model, 84.6 percent of officers agreed with this statement. Their opinion appears to show widespread support for the possession and possible use of taser by officers in the course of their law enforcement duties. They believe that having this tool provides for their safety and keeps unruly subjects away from them so that they do not have to engage in manual combat tactics or resort to pulling their firearm.

A third question on the instrument asked officers their level of agreement with the statement: "Based on your experience would you say that being equipped with an (ECD) taser makes you more confident in your ability to control noncompliant or combative suspects?" Table 24 provides the results for this question.

Table 24: Officers Confidence in Use of Taser for Controlling Noncompliant or Combative Suspects

Level of Agreement	N	Percentage
Strongly Disagree	7	5.4
Disagree	16	12.3
Neutral	4	3.1
Agree	55	42.3
Strongly Agree	48	36.9
Total	130	100.0

* Percentages may not equal 100% due to rounding error

As with the previous questions, the officers in this survey expressed confidence in the taser and its ability to help them control combative or noncompliant suspects. Overall, 79.2 percent agreed or strongly agreed with this statement. This level of support was expected; however, it was not expected that 17.7 percent, or approximately 1 in 5 officers, did not feel the same way. It may be that these officers were involved in an incident that led to a disciplinary or citizen complaint issue. Another possibility is that these officers do not believe that tasers are an effective LTL weapon. Clearly, this is a question that needs to be explored in future research.

A fourth question on the instrument asked officers their level of agreement to the statement "Based on your experience would you say that the change in agency policy relating to placement of the taser (ECD) on the resistance and response continuum makes you more inclined to other use-of-force options prior to deploying an (ECD)?" Table 25 presents the results for this question and the officers' level of agreement.

Table 25: Officer's Opinions on Using Other Force Options Prior to Using a Taser

Level of Agreement	N	Percentage
Strongly Disagree	14	10.8
Disagree	31	23.8
Neutral	3	2.3
Agree	48	36.9
Strongly Agree	33	25.4
Total	130	100.0

* Percentages may not equal 100% due to rounding error

A majority of the respondents responded to this question affirmatively, with 62.3 percent stating that they are more inclined to use other force options prior to deploying a taser. However, 34.6 percent stated that this change in organizational policy made little difference to them regarding whether or not they would consider other options in the field. Thus, it may be possible that many officers, or at least about a third of the officers in this sample, do not pay heed to the placement of tasers in the Use-of-Force Continuum.

A synthesis of these survey responses indicates a strong preference for the taser as a use-of-force method and a perception that it provides a significant measure of safety for officers during use-of-force encounters. However, the results also demonstrate that officers perceive that the policy change makes them more inclined to use other use-of-force options prior to deploying a taser. It is also undetermined whether officers believe that the policy change decreases their ability to control suspects who are resistive or noncompliant.

Based on these survey responses, the research hypothesis cannot be rejected. These findings support that officers perceive that the change in organizational policy relating to taser placement on the Use-of-Force Continuum increases their risk of injury during a use-of-force incident. The archival data related to the frequency of injury to officers revealed that there was an increase in the frequency of injury to officers after the change in agency policy. The analysis of officers' perceptions reveals that they believe that the policy change increases the risk of injury to them during a use-of-force encounter. For this research question, the perceptions of the officers do in fact match the findings of the archival data analysis.

Research Question 7: Officer Perception of Increased Risk of Harm to Suspects as a Result of Organizational Policy Change

Research question 7 examined if officers believe that the change in organizational policy relating to the authorized level on the Use-of-Force Continuum for taser use has increased the risk of harm to suspects in a use-of-force encounter.

It is important to examine officer perceptions related to the change in risk to suspects as a result of the policy change as this may have an effect on how often officers deploy the taser and their level of confidence with it as a use-of-force method. If officers perceive that the more stringent guidelines of the policy change may cause more severe injuries to suspects, they may again defer to other use-of-force methods to avoid inflicting injuries and/or generating citizen complaints. As in the previous research question, it is important to compare the archival data on the frequency and severity of injury to suspects to see if it matches with the archival data form use-of-force encounters.

HO_7: Officers express no preference as to whether the change in organizational policy relating to when the taser can be used increases the risk of harm to suspects in a use-of-force encounter.

$H1_7$: Officers perceive that the change in organizational policy relating to when the taser can be used increases the risk of harm to suspects in a use-of-force encounter.

Two questions from the survey instrument were asked to capture respondents' perceptions relating to the increased risk of harm to suspects resulting from the organizational policy change. Officers were asked for their level of agreement to the statement: "The policy change relating to placement of the taser (ECD) on the resistance and response continuum increases the risk of harm to suspect(s) during a use-of-force incident." Table 26 presents the results for this question.

Table 26: Officer's Opinions on Change in Policy Increasing the Potential Harm to Suspects

Level of Agreement	N	Percentage
Strongly Disagree	54	41.5
Disagree	33	25.4
Neutral	8	6.2
Agree	25	19.2
Strongly Agree	10	7.7
Total	130	100.0

* Percentages may not equal 100% due to rounding error

A majority of the respondents, 66.9% (87) believed that the change in policy did not negatively affect the safety of citizens involved in use-of-force encounters. However, (35) 26.9% of the respondents felt that increasing the level of resistance before tasers could be used increased the likelihood that citizens may be seriously harmed. While this percentage is higher than what was found in the previous few runs, it may be that some officers are extremely well acclimated to electronic control devices such as tasers and believe that limiting their use is likely to mean that officers are more likely to be involved in hand-to-hand combat situations, where there is a higher likelihood of serious injury.

An additional question asked respondents for their level of agreement to the statement "Based on your experience would you say that the change in agency policy relating to placement of the taser (ECD) on the resistance and response continuum has increased the chances that a suspect confrontation will escalate to deadly force." Table 27 presents the results for this question.

Table 27: Officers' Perceptions that Restriction on Use of Tasers Will Increase Chances that a Confrontation Will Escalate to Deadly Force

Level of Agreement	N	Percentage
Strongly Disagree	35	26.9
Disagree	30	23.1
Neutral	19	14.6
Agree	36	27.7
Strongly Agree	10	7.7
	130	100.0

* Percentages may not equal 100% due to rounding error

Officers in this survey were somewhat ambivalent as to whether or not the movement of the use of tasers on the Use-of-Force Continuum was likely to increase the chances that a given police-citizen encounter would escalate to a deadly force situation. Previous survey data supports that a majority of officers support the use of tasers for dealing with unruly suspects and like to have them in their complement of tools, it is likely that deadly force situations arise so infrequently that it may be unreasonable to expect any consensus of opinion on such a rare event. Although, when you examine all of those that disagreed (35.4%) and those that agreed (50%), it is clear that, on the average, officers do consider these ECDs as a valuable tool in their arsenal and one that may prevent a use-of-force situation from escalating.

Based on these survey responses, the null hypothesis is not rejected. This finding supports the notion that officers believe that the change in organizational policy relating to taser placement on the Use-of-Force Continuum does not increase risk of injury to suspects during a use-of-force incident. The archival data on the severity of injury to suspects revealed no difference in either the frequency or severity of injuries to suspects after the policy change. For this research question, the officers' perceptions appear to match the archival data findings.

Research Question 8: Officer Belief that the Placement of Taser on the Use-of-Force Continuum is Appropriate for Most Use-of-Force Encounters

Research question 8 examined the question of appropriate placement of the taser on the Use-of-Force Continuum for most encounters. It is important to examine officer beliefs related to the placement of the taser on the Use-of-Force Continuum as a result of the policy change as this may have an effect on their level of confidence with the taser as a use-of-force method. If officers feel constrained by the more stringent guidelines of the policy change and do not believe that the policy change appropriately places the taser on the Use-of-Force Continuum for most encounters, they may opt not to deploy tasers in favor of other use-of-force methods.

For this research question, the research hypotheses are:

$H0_8$: Officers express no preference as to whether the change in organizational policy relating to when the taser can be used places the taser on the Use-of-Force Continuum appropriately for most use-of-force encounters.

$H1_8$: Officers perceive that the change in organizational policy relating to when the taser can be used places the taser on the Use-of-Force Continuum appropriately for most use-of-force encounters.

One question from the survey instrument captured the respondents' perceptions regarding whether the change in organizational policy that increased the level of suspect resistance required to deploy tasers was appropriate for most use-of-force encounters. Officers were asked their level of agreement to the statement that "The placement of taser (ECD) at a level IV (active resistance) on the resistance and response continuum is appropriate for most use-of-force incidents." Table 28 presents the results for this question.

Table 28: Officer Belief that the Placement of Taser on the Use-of-Force Continuum at Active Resistance Level is Appropriate for Most Use-of-Force Encounters

Level of Agreement	N	Percentage
Strongly Disagree	9	6.9
Disagree	24	18.5
Neutral	3	2.3
Agree	55	42.3
Strongly Agree	39	30.0
	130	100.0

* Percentages may not equal 100% due to rounding error

A majority of the respondents, 72.3% (94), agreed or strongly agreed that placement of taser on the Use-of-Force Continuum at a level IV (active resistance) is appropriate for most use-of-force encounters. This indicates that a majority of the officers supported the policy that places the taser at a level on the Use-of-Force Continuum requiring active resistance for most use-of-force incidents.

Based on these survey responses, the null research hypothesis is rejected. The results of this survey question supports that officers believe that the change in organizational policy relating to taser placement on the Use-of-Force Continuum places the taser at an appropriate level of force for most use-of-force encounters.

SUMMARY

This chapter presents an analysis of the data and research hypotheses related to the effect of organizational policy change on taser use and effectiveness. Table 29 below displays a listing of the research questions and related findings. Furthermore, an analysis of the archival data suggests that after the policy change that raised the authorized level on the Use-of-Force Continuum for deploying tasers, the frequency of taser use decreased. As expected, the levels of suspect resistance after the policy change increased. An analysis of suspect injuries revealed that there was no change in the frequency or level of severity of suspect injuries in the posttest period. The frequency of injuries to officers did not increase after the policy change.

Survey response data from officers revealed that officers perceive an increased risk to themselves as a result of the organizational policy change. However, officers perceive a decreased risk of harm to suspects as a result of the policy change. Officers expressed a belief that the organizational change placing the taser at a higher level on the Use-of-Force Continuum is appropriate for most use-of-force encounters.

A discussion and summary of these findings is presented in the next chapter as well as conclusions and recommendations for additional research.

Table 29: Summary of Research Questions and Findings

Research Question	Subject	Accept or Reject Hypothesis	Summary of Findings
Question 1	Frequency of taser use	Reject Null Hypothesis	Frequency decreased
Question 2	Level of suspect resistance	Reject Null Hypothesis	Suspect level of resistance increased
Question 3	Frequency of injury to suspects	Fail to Reject Null Hypothesis	No change in frequency of injury to suspects
Question 4	Severity of Injury to suspects	Fail to Reject Null Hypothesis	No change in severity of injury to suspects
Question 5	Frequency of injury to officers	Fail to Reject Null Hypothesis	No change in frequency of injury to officers
Question 6	Perceived risk of injury to officer	Accept Hypothesis	Officers perceive increase in risk to themselves
Question 7	Perceived increased harm to suspects	Fail to Reject Null Hypothesis	Officers do not perceive increase in risk to suspects
Question 8	Placement of taser on the Use-of-Force Continuum is appropriate for most use-of-force encounters	Reject Null Hypothesis	Officers believe that placement is appropriate for most use-of-force encounters

CHAPTER FIVE:
Conclusions and Future Implications

This work examined one agency's experiences with organizational policy changes regarding taser placement on the Use-of-Force Continuum and officers' perceptions of taser effectiveness. Two different time periods were identified for analysis, constituting one year prior to the policy change and one year after the policy change. In addition, a survey instrument captured officers' perceptions of taser use and effectiveness as it relates to the organizational policy change, with additional survey questions related to the Use-of-Force Continuum as it relates to the taser.

By examining both archival data and officers' responses to survey questions, a clearer understanding of the influence of policy changes on taser use and effectiveness has emerged. This analysis was designed to see if officers' perceptions coincide with the reality depicted in the archival data from use-of-force encounters. A comparison of the results of the archival data analysis and the officers' perceptions generates important findings to stimulate discussion and further investigation. This type of examination will produce a more comprehensive investigation of the research questions and add academic rigor and value to the study's findings and conclusions.

KEY FINDINGS

When and how often police use tasers remain a focus for public debate and criticism. In the face of this criticism, many police agencies have chosen to modify their Use-of-Force continuum policies relating to when tasers can be deployed. Most of these changes have restricted officers in when and how to use tasers. While this change may seem prudent from a management perspective, it is not an academic solution to what is a more complex problem. Most use of force incidents cannot be easily classified into distinct categories. Each incident produces its own distinct variables and influences. Without proper examination and investigation, a policy decision related to these events could create unintended consequences for both suspects and officers. These consequences could have serious implications for police agencies, individual officers and suspects. This research is designed to thoroughly examine how policy changes related to use of force ultimately influenced a variety of variables related to the taser use.

The effect on the frequency of taser use after the policy change was a primary question of this research study. A Z-test for the difference in proportions was applied to the number of arrests, the number of calls for service::arrest, and the total number of uses of force in the year before the policy change and one year after. These results revealed tasers were used more frequently in the one-year period prior to the policy change. This finding also substantiates a reduction of taser use in the one-year period after the policy change. Therefore, the findings support that the change in organizational policy related to taser placement on the Use-of-Force Continuum did have a significant effect on the frequency of taser use. This change resulted in a measurable reduction in the frequency of taser use after the change in organizational policy.

The injury of suspects in a use-of-force encounter is also a primary concern of police agencies. For this reason, the effect on frequency of injuries to suspects after the policy change was also examined. An analysis of the archival data suggests that there is no significant difference in the frequency of injury to suspects after the change in policy.

The severity of injuries to suspects was also a primary focus of this research. The effect on severity of suspects' injuries during use-of-force encounters after the policy change was also examined. The results indicate that there was no significant difference in the severity of suspect injuries after the change in organizational policy.

Another important component of police use-of-force is the protection of officers during use-of-force encounters. Specifically, this research examined if injuries to officers occurred more frequently after the policy change. Data analysis results support that there was no difference in the frequency of injury to officers after the change in policy. The numbers of injuries to officers did not change significantly, as organizational policy limited the use of tasers to only those encounters involving higher levels of suspect resistance.

The level of suspect resistance in a use-of-force encounter is the primary determinant of the amount of force police officers can use to counter it. This force response is mandated by the Use-of-Force Continuum. For this reason, the effect on levels of suspect resistance after the organizational policy change was also examined. The results of these analyses support the findings that there is a significant difference in the level of suspect resistance encountered by officers after the change in organizational policy. These findings indicate that levels of suspect resistance increased significantly after the policy change. Based on the structure of the Use-of-Force Continuum and the purpose for its existence, this finding is not unexpected. The Use-of-Force Continuum is a tool that guides the application of force, in incremental and proportional levels, to raise or lower force levels as the level of suspect resistance changes during an encounter. Therefore, since the policy change raised the authorized level on the Use-of-Force Continuum for when a taser can be deployed, it is only logical that suspect resistance levels would also be greater. Officers are prohibited by their agency use-of-force policy to deploy tasers when less than the authorized level of suspect resistance is encountered. This finding supports that the organizational policy change produced the desired result, which was limiting taser use in lower-level (passive resistance) encounters.

The severity of suspect injury also was significantly influenced by the level of suspect resistance. This finding is reasonable based on the nature of use-of-force encounters and the escalation of force used to overcome resistance. As the level of resistance encountered by officers increased, so did the severity of the injuries incurred when force was applied to control that resistance.

Several other control variables were also found to be significant. The number of primary officers involved in the use-of-force incident was found to be significant. This would indicate that the greater number of officers involved in the incident, the greater the influence on the level of suspect resistance. Given the fact that multiple officers are often sent to more serious and potentially more violent encounters, this finding is logical and expected. The number of suspects involved in the incident was also significant. This finding also seems intuitive since the greater the number of suspects encountered in the incident, the more influence on the level of suspect resistance would be expected. A greater number of suspects involved in an encounter would indicate larger-scale disturbances or more serious crimes involving multiple offenders.

Officers' perceptions relating to the potential of increased risk to them posed by the policy change were captured in a survey instrument. Responses from these survey questions support that officers' believe that:

1. The change in policy increased their risk of harm during a use-of-force encounter.
2. Being equipped with a taser makes them safer when working as a police officer.
3. Being equipped with a taser makes them more confident in their ability to control noncompliant or combative suspects.
4. The policy change makes them more inclined to use other use-of-force options prior to deploying a taser.

These findings support a strong preference from respondents for the taser as a use-of-force weapon and a perception that it provides a significant measure of protection for officers during use-of-force encounters. Despite this expressed confidence in the taser and the Use-of-Force Continuum as a guide for its deployment, a majority of the respondent's still perceive that the policy change increased their risk of harm during a use-of-force encounter. Respondents also indicated that they are more inclined to use other use-of-force options before deploying the taser.

Officers' perceptions relating to the potential of increased risks to suspects posed by the policy change were also examined. Two survey questions were asked to capture officers' perceptions relating to the increased risk to suspects from the change in agency policy. The officers believe that the policy change relating to placement of the taser on the Use-of-Force Continuum increases the risk of harm to suspects during a use-of-force encounter. Officers were then asked if the change in agency policy has increased the chances that a suspect confrontation will escalate to deadly force. Some ambiguity among respondents was noted regarding the effect of the policy change and the potential for an encounter to escalate to the use of deadly force as a result of the change in agency policy. Due to the infrequent and random nature of deadly force events, this finding is not unexpected. These results support the finding that officers do not perceive that the change in policy relating to the placement of the taser on the Use-of-Force Continuum increases risk of injury to suspects during a use-of-force incident.

Officers' perceptions concerning whether the policy change that raised the authorized level of suspect resistance required for deploying tasers was appropriate for most use-of-force encounters was the focus of this survey research. Survey responses support the finding that officers believe the change in policy places the taser at an appropriate level of force for most use-of-force encounters. Additional survey responses support that, in general, officers believe the Use-of-Force Continuum makes their job less dangerous.

THEORETICAL IMPLICATIONS

The theoretical framework for this study was based on the work of Thacher and Rein (2004). Their theory of value conflict and policy change explicates government's tendency to balance competing goals or striking trade-offs among values. They define values-oriented casuistry, or rationalization, as a form of moral taxonomy that aids in values balancing.

The dilemma faced by police officers when use-of-force is indicated is that the placement of tasers in the Use-of-Force Continuum often conflicts with the officers' core value of trying to balance safety for all. In these situations, officers tend to use the taser when they see fit, even if this conflicts with agency policy. The testing of the officers' ability to balance these values with when to use this type of non-lethal force was the focus of this research study. The Use-of-Force Continuum and the policies that guide its use are the mechanism used by police to manage use-of-force encounters. The policies that guide taser use and, more specifically, the Use-of-Force Continuum attempt to balance competing values of the safety of the public, including suspects, and the safety of police officers. The findings of this study indicate that, by changing the placement of taser on the Use-of-Force Continuum, the balance of safety between officers and suspects relating to the frequency of injuries was essentially unchanged as a result of the policy change. The policy change had no measured effect on the frequency of injuries to either suspects or officers.

As expected, the levels of suspect resistance encountered by officers increased as a result of the policy change. Unfortunately, no measure of the change in the level of severity of injuries to officers could be obtained from the archival data to conclusively resolve this question. The frequency of taser use decreased as a result of the policy change, which resulted in an increased level of safety for officers and suspects. In effect, the policy change reduced the probability that tasers would be deployed in use-of-force encounters during the post-change study period.

These conclusions support the finding that the change in organizational policy relating to placement of the taser on the

Use-of-Force Continuum has achieved the desired effect of increased safety to citizens. By increasing the level of suspect resistance required to authorize taser deployment, the frequency of taser use declined. This finding would seem to be supported by the theory of value balancing as advanced by Thacher and Rein (2004). The net effect of this change may be increased safety for the public by reducing taser use without significantly increasing risk to officers.

SUMMARY

After an analysis of the archival data, the findings suggest that after the policy change that raised the authorized level on the Use-of-Force Continuum for deploying taser, the frequency of taser use by officers decreased, while the levels of suspect resistance encountered by officers after the policy change increased. The analysis of suspect injuries revealed no change in either the frequency or severity of injuries to suspects after the policy change. The frequency of injuries to officers also did not increase after the policy change.

Survey response data from officers revealed that, while officers perceive an increased risk of harm to themselves as a result of the organizational policy change, they did not perceive an increased risk of harm to suspects. Officers expressed a belief that the organizational change is appropriate for most use-of-force encounters. Given the existing literature on police culture and behavior, this finding is unexpected and compelling. As prior research has revealed, police officers do not universally accept organizational policy changes (Crank and Langworthy 1992; Lingamneni, 1979). Officers have demonstrated a particular aversion to specific policy changes that limit the use of police discretion. This research study's findings would seem to contradict this conventional finding and lend support to the premise that officers will accept some forms of change when practical experience and application are factored into the formation of their perceptions.

Comparing archival data findings and the officer survey responses yielded an interesting finding. The analysis of archival data depicts no change in the frequency or severity of injuries to suspects as result of the policy change. There was no statistically significant increase in the frequency of injuries to officers after the policy change. Survey responses from officers reveal a belief that the policy change that altered the placement of the taser on the Use-of-Force Continuum increases their risk of injury. However, this belief is not supported by the findings from the analysis of the archival data. These beliefs may emphasize a level of frustration on the part of officers, who perceive the policy change as limiting their discretion, and officers may see this limitation as weakening their ability to act promptly and decisively in a use-of-force encounter.

The analysis of archival data reveals that the severity of injuries to suspects after the policy change did not change. Officer survey responses also indicate a perception that there is no increased risk of injury to suspects from the change in policy. It appears that the officers' perceptions that there is no increased risk to suspects as a result of the policy change are supported by the archival data.

STUDY LIMITATIONS

This research study produced a number of relevant findings relating to organizational policy change and taser use. This study uses methods of acquiring data through research of related literature, examination of use-of-force documentation, review of related agency documents, and analysis of officer survey responses. However, several limitations and methodological shortcomings were apparent in this study. This method of analysis is limited in the following ways:

This research study is limited to the use of taser weapons by a single police agency. Because a single police agency was used for analysis, some aspects of this research may not be generalizable to the greater law enforcement population. Every effort was made to insure that OPD was in fact representative of other mid size police agencies.

The OPD's policies and practices regarding deployment of taser weapons are unique to their organization, and they may alter the way the data was interpreted. Certain terminology and formatting had to be generalized to correspond with more mainstream use-of-force terms and context. This was only done to add clarity and to inform the reader.

Data related to the injuries to suspects relied on the accurate documentation of the injuries by the investigating police supervisor. The level of detail as to the extent and description of injuries can be subjective and difficult to categorize. No details were provided as to the severity of injuries to officers on the use-of-force forms. Every effort was made to maintain consistency in recording the responses related to the extent of injury recorded on the use-of-force form; however, this is largely based on the observations of the reporting officer.

The use of self-reported data by officers in use-of-force incidents can lead to exaggeration of certain aspects of an event, such as the level of resistance exhibited by the suspect or accurately describing the injuries to a suspect during an encounter. This limitation has been noted in previous studies that use archival use-of-force data.

Similarly, the categorizing of incident types for the levels of resistance encountered and for the seriousness of the threat encountered relied on accurate descriptions and categorizing of the incidents that led to the use-of-force incident. Every effort was made to consistently document and classify these data.

For the survey research portion of the study, the principal limitation was the low response rate to the survey instrument. The response rate for the electronic survey was 39%, or 130 respondents out of 333 who were contacted and invited to participate. While this response rate was deemed acceptable, a larger response rate would be more desirable and add rigor to the study findings and conclusions. It is unclear exactly why the officer response rate was low. One can speculate that officers are reluctant to state their opinions about such a controversial topic.

It could also be that officers feel that their use-of-force incidents already are scrutinized by the public and commanders, so why should they add to the debate by stating their opinions, which may be in conflict with agency policies and further reduce their discretion in use-of-force incidents.

The effect of the public controversy and the associated media reports that preceded the change in policy at OPD cannot be ignored. It is impossible to accurately measure the effect that this may have had on the frequency of taser use by officers during the identified analysis periods. The survey response data indicates awareness by officers of the public controversy and a finding that they believe that the change places taser use appropriately on the Use-of-Force Continuum for most encounters. The inability to measure the effect of this scrutiny on taser deployments in the archival data analysis remains a limitation of this research.

FUTURE IMPLICATIONS

When and how police use tasers in use of force incidents remains a focal point for public debate and media scrutiny. The advent and proliferation of video technology in law enforcement has provided the mechanism to bring any police use of force incident into a public forum via the mainstream media. This kind of exposure often without the benefit of explanation or reflection incites public opinion and has the potential to influence police policymakers and political leaders to modify police use of force policies and restrict police discretion. These changes are often created in a vacuum separate from research or empirical analysis.

This type of research provides benefits in three separate areas related to police use-of-force. These areas are civil liability, training, and policy development in other high liability areas.

Many police agencies have chosen to address these issues by modifying their Use-of-Force Continuum policy relating to when tasers can be deployed. Other agencies have abandoned the Use-of-Force Continuum all together, in favor of a more legalistic model based on prevailing court rulings. The main goal of any organizational policy related to use-of-force is protect both officers and suspects while reducing civil liability for the agency. The more legalistic models of use-of-force policy may shield agencies from potential civil liability but also could expose either officers or the public to increased risk of injury. These models rely heavily on officer training as the guiding force for decision making in a use of force incident. Most use-of-force incidents develop rapidly in very fluid environments. Officers must make split second decisions about the level of force that is appropriate to counter suspect resistance. The Use-of-Force Continuum requires officers to choose only the appropriate level of force to counter the resistance being shown by the suspect. Some opponents of use-of-force continuums posit this causes hesitation or confusion by officers that could result in officer injuries or the use of excessive force to subdue a suspect. What is lacking in the extant literature is more empirical study of existing use of force data related to the variables that effect these use of force incidents. Additional research using this data would provide a basis for more informed and purposeful policy development.

The replication of this research study using a larger sample, longer period, or multiple police agencies could yield additional valuable data and findings. These study options would also increase generalizability, allowing for application to a larger law enforcement population. It would also be valuable to solicit the opinions of suspects and the general population regarding being exposed to tasers or witnessing someone being exposed to the taser in a use-of-force incident. This qualitative data might provide valuable insight and further explicate the use of police tactics from the perspective of offenders, as well as the public observing such incidents.

Most areas of high liability for police rely on a training component to ensure that officers are indoctrinated in the proper application of policy. Limited research has been done to assess the effectiveness of training in achieving desired outcomes in these areas. This type of research study could be used to evaluate and validate training in these areas. By identifying variables that influence officer and suspect behavior in incidents common themes or characteristics could be identified. These themes could be incorporated in training programs to provide instruction that would allow officers to make better decisions related to use of force or the high liability area that is the subject of the training. Studies could then be conducted to determine the post training effects using actual data from incidents.

An additional area that could benefit from this type of research is policy development in other high liability areas such as vehicle apprehension or other types of use-of-force. Studies could be conducted that incorporate the use of chemical spray or impact weapons and organizational policy changes. These findings could be compared and analyzed for changes in outcomes or effectiveness.

Applying this study template to other types of organizational policy changes to evaluate positive outcomes or effectiveness could provide useful data. Several areas such as vehicle pursuit, police tactics, or deadly force issues could be examined using this method. This type of research could yield valuable data to guide police decision makers when contemplating changes to policy and procedures related to high liability areas, such as use-of-force and vehicle pursuit. These studies could yield valuable findings and add to the growing body of research on police use-of-force.

OPD Resistance and Response Continuum

Resistance and Response Continuum
Orlando Police Department

Suspect's Resistance	Employee's Response
LEVEL I – INDICATORS OF RESISTANCE	EMPLOYEE'S PRESENCE
Non-verbal cues indicating subject's demeanor and attitude coupled with an apparent readiness to resist.	The employee's attitude and demeanor and their lawful right to be where they are.
LEVEL II – VERBAL RESISTANCE The subject's verbal responses indicating non-compliance and unwillingness to cooperate	VERBAL DIRECTIONS The employee's verbal communications that specifically direct the actions of the subject and offer the opportunity for compliance.
LEVEL III – PASSIVE RESISTANCE The subject fails to obey verbal direction preventing the member from taking lawful action.	SOFT CONTROL The employee applies techniques that have a minimal potential for injury to the subject, if the subject resists the technique.
LEVEL IV – ACTIVE RESISTANCE The subject's actions are intended to facilitate an escape or prevent an arrest. The action is not likely to cause injury.	HARD CONTROL The member applies techniques that could result in greater injury to the subject, if the subject resists their application by the member.

Suspect's Resistance	Employee's Response
LEVEL V – AGGRESSIVE RESISTANCE The subject has battered, or is about to batter a person/member and the subject's action is likely to cause injury.	INTENSIFIED TECHNIQUES Those techniques necessary to overcome the actions of the subject, short of deadly force. If the subject resists or continues to resist these techniques there is a strong probability of injury being incurred by the subject.
LEVEL VI – DEADLY FORCE RESISTANCE The subject's actions are likely to cause death or great bodily harm to the member or another person	DEADLY FORCE Member's actions may result in death or great bodily harm to the subject.

RESISTANCE AND RESPONSE CONTINUUM
(TECHNIQUE GUIDELINES)
ORLANDO POLICE DEPARTMENT

EMPLOYEE'S PRESENCE	◆ Lawful presence ◆ Attitude and demeanor ◆ Identification of authority
VERBAL DIRECTIONS	◆ Commands to direct subject action ◆ Notification of arrest ◆ Opportunity to comply

SOFT CONTROL TECHNIQUES	◆ Techniques having minimal potential of injury if resisted by a subject
	  o Pressure points
	  o Wrist locks
	  o Arm bars
	  o Compression techniques
	  o Chemical agents

HARD CONTROL TECHNIQUES	◆ Techniques having a greater potential of injury if resisted by a subject
	  o Forearm/knee/open and closed hand strikes
	  o Strikes with the baton
	  o Kicks
	  o Takedowns
	  o Head locks
	  o Impact weapons
	  o Tire deflation devices
	  o Electronic control devices (TASER)

INTENSIFIED TECHNIQUES	◆ Techniques necessary to overcome actions of a subject short of deadly force.
DEADLY FORCE	◆ Techniques that may result in death or great bodily harm to the subject ◆ The application of deadly force is not limited to the use of a firearm, and may include application of other techniques and/or weapons.

EMPLOYEE/SUBJECT FACTORS AND SPECIAL CIRCUMSTANCES	
EMPLOYEE/ SUBJECT FACTORS TO BE CONSIDERED: • Age • Sex • Size • Skill level • Multiple subjects or employees	SPECIAL CIRCUMSTANCES: • Mental incapacity • Close proximity to firearm or weapon • Special knowledge • Injury or exhaustion (member/suspect) • Disability • Imminent danger • Availability of weapons • Arrestee's level of agitation • Alcohol/drug influence • Arrestee handcuffed

OPD Defensive Tactics Form

ORLANDO POLICE DEPARTMENT

DEFENSIVE TACTICS FORM

NOTE: FOR INTERNAL USE ONLY – UNDER NO CIRCUMSTANCES SHALL THIS FORM BE FILED IN CENTRAL RECORDS.

TO: CHIEF OF POLICE
ORLANDO POLICE DEPARTMENT

Complaint # _____
Sector: _____
District #: _____
Grid #: _____

FROM:

Name _____ Employee # _____

INVOLVED EMPLOYEE'S SECTION MANAGER:

1. Incident Location: _____ Date: _____ Time: _____

2. Time Supervisor Notified: _____ On Scene: _____ Other: _____

Name of Manager Notified: _____ Time Notified _____

Type Incident: _____

3. Offense Charged: _____

134

Offender #1 Name: _____

A   Race _____ Sex _____ DOB _____ Height _____ Weight _____

B.   Address _____ City _____ State _____

C.   Physical condition prior to incident (i.e., intoxication, prior injuries): _____

D.   Subsequent apparent injuries: _____

E.   Photographs of injuries: Digital Image ☐ 35 mm ☐

      None taken ☐ Why? _____

F.   Medical treatment of offender: Yes ☐   No ☐   Refused ☐

      If Yes, where? _____ By whom? _____

      Date: _____ Time: _____

Offender #2 Name: _____

A.   Race _____ Sex _____ DOB _____ Height _____ Weight _____

B.   Address _____ City _____ State _____

C.   Physical condition prior to incident (i.e., intoxication, prior injuries): _____

_____

_____

D.   Subsequent apparent injuries: _____

E.   Photographs of injuries: 35 mm ☐ Digital Image ☐

      None taken ☐   Why? _____

_____

135

F. Medical treatment of offender: Yes ☐   No ☐   Refused ☐
    If Yes, where? _____   By whom? _____
    Date: _____   Time: _____

4. Employees involved: _____ # Battered: _____ # Injured: _____

    List principal employees in order of their degree of physical involvement:

    Note: For the purposes of this policy and procedure, a principal employee is: "Any employee who encounters physical resistance from a subject and must use greater force than controlling techniques or restraint holds to overcome it."

	Name	R/S	DOH	Age	Employee #
A.					
B.					
C.					
D.					

Attach copy of Charging Affidavit and/or Incident Report

136

5. Implements used by employees:

	ECD TASER Cartridge #	Chemical Agents	Impact Weapon	K-9	Stop Sticks/ Tire Deflation Device		Specify Implement and Explain Employee's Involvement
A.							
B.							
C.							
D.							

6. Physical technique used by employees.

	Tackle / Take Down	Hands	Other	Specify Technique and Explain Employee's Involvement
A.				
B.				
C.				
D.				

7. List <u>assisting</u> employees and their physical involvement:

	Name	Employee #	Involvement
A.			
B.			
C.			
D.			

8. Witnesses

	Name	Address	Phone #
A.			
B.			
C.			
D.			

Defensive Tactics Form - Continued

SUPERVISOR'S NARRATIVE (Include [1] general circumstances; [2] specific resistance encountered; [3] physical techniques utilized; [4] extent of injuries incurred; [5] who incurred and inflicted the injuries; [6] statement of witnesses; [7] when applicable, appropriate manager was notified, [8] supervisor's endorsement; and, [9] a statement whether the force used was in keeping with policy.)

_____

_____

_____

_____

_____

_____

_____

_____

	Approve	Disapprove (Attach Dissent)	
Reporting Supervisor	☐	☐	_____ Date
Training Supervisor	☐ Technique/Tactic Used	☐	_____ Date
Training Section Cmdr.	☐	☐	_____ Date
Employee's Supervisor (If different than reporting supervisor)	☐	☐	_____ Date
Section Commander	☐	☐	_____ Date
Division Commander	☐	☐	_____ Date
Bureau Commander	☐	☐	_____ Date

OPD Officer Survey Instrument

Organizational Policy Change and Taser Effectiveness – Officer Survey (OPD)

1. Organizational Policy Change and Taser Effectiveness Survey – Informed Consent

Dear Officer,

You are among several Orlando police officers who have been selected to participate in a confidential online taser use survey. This survey is part of a research study related to how organizational policy changes on the placement of taser on the use of force continuum have effected taser use and effectiveness. Your participation and honest answers are crucial for assessing how this policy change related to the placement of the taser on your agency's use of force continuum has effected taser use and your safety.

- The following questions ask for your perceptions about the use of taser before and after your agency's change in the placement on the use of force matrix.

- You may also be asked questions related to your general perceptions of your working environment as a police officer.

- This survey is completely voluntary. You may choose not to participate or not to answer any specific questions. You may skip any question you are not comfortable answering,. You can decline to participate in this survey for any reason. There are no anticipated risks.

- The survey is confidential and some of the questions are personal in nature. You can be assured that your individual responses and your identities will only be known to the researcher and will not be divulged. The survey results will be captured electronically through a software program and will be password protected for privacy.

- This study examines law enforcement taser use, beliefs, and attitudes. The information will be used to evaluate the effect of policy changes related to the placement of the taser on the use of force continuum.

- The online survey will take approximately twenty minutes to complete. You can complete the survey right now, or anytime up until 09/;01/2007.
- Your privacy and research records will be kept confidential to the extent of the law. Authorized research personnel, the UCF Institutional Review Board and its staff, and other individuals, acting on behalf of UCF, may inspect the records from this research project.
- The results of this study may be published. However, the data obtained from you will be combined with data fro others in the publication. The published results will not include your name or any other information that would personally identify you in any way.
- If you have any questions about this survey or the research study being conducted you can contact the primary researcher, Michael Miller by phone at (407)254-7226, or via email at Michael.Miller@ocfl.net. The faculty supervisor for this research is Dr. Stephen Holmes. He can be contacted at (407)823-2211 or via email at sholmes@mail.ucf.edu.
- Research at the University of Central Florida involving human participants is carried out under the oversight of the Institutional Review Board (IRB). Questions or concerns about research participants' rights may be directed to UCF Institutional Review Board Office at the University of Central Florida, Office of Research and Commercialization, 12201 Research Parkway, Suite 501, Orlando, FL 32826-3246. The phone numbers are 407-823-2901 or 407-882-2276.

Thank you for taking the time and effort to complete this survey. I sincerely appreciate your participation. Your time and effort in helping us gather information will ultimately help law enforcement policy makers evaluate the effectiveness of policy changes on taser use and officer safety issues.

Sincerely,

Michael E. Miller, Doctoral Candidate
University of Central Florida
PhD in Public Affairs Program

Faculty Supervisor:
Dr. Stephen Holmes, Associate Dean
University of Central Florida
Department Criminal Justice and Legal Studies

2, Officer demographics and characteristics

1. What is your gender:
    - ○ Female
    - ○ Male

2. What is your race or ethnicity?
    - ○ White
    - ○ Black (or African American)
    - ○ Latino
    - ○ Asian
    - ○ Other

        If other please specify

3. What year were you born?_____

4. What is the highest level of education you have completed?
    - ○ less than a high school diploma
    - ○ High school diploma or GED
    - ○ some junior college, but did not earn a degree
    - ○ Associates degree
    - ○ more than two years of college but did not earn a degree
    - ○ Bachelors degree
    - ○ some graduate courses, but did not earn a graduate degree
    - ○ Graduate degree

5. What year did you become a law enforcement officer? _____

6. What year did you join the Orlando Police Department? _____

7.   Have you ever worked for another law enforcement agency?

     O   Yes

     O   No

          If yes, please state where

          _____

8.   My rank in the Police Department from June 1, 2003 – July 1, 2005 was

     _____.
     (If you were promoted during this period which rank did you hold for the
     majority of this period?

     O   Police Officer

     O   Master Police Officer

     O   Detective

     O   Sergeant

     O   Lieutenant

9.   My unit assignment in the Police Department from June 1, 2003 – July 1,
     2005 was _____.
     (If you were transferred during this period which unit were you assigned to
     for the majority of this period?

     O   Patrol

     O   Tactical

     O   Detectives

     O   Narcotics

     O   Motors

3. Organizational policy changes and taser use questions

The following questions deal specifically with issues related to the organizational policy change by your agency in June 2004 which raised the level in the resistance and response continuum for taser use from Level III (passive resistance) to Level IV (active resistance). Please indicate how strongly you agree or disagree with the statement below.

10. The policy changes relating to placement of the taser (ECD) on the resistance and response continuum increase the risk of harm to you from suspects during a use of force incident?

O	O	O	O	O
Strongly disagree	Uncertain	Disagree somewhat	Agree somewhat	Strongly agree

11. The policy change relating to placement of the taser (ECD) on a resistance and response continuum increased the risk of harm to suspect(s) from a taser deployment during a use of force agreement?

O	O	O	O	O
Strongly disagree	Uncertain	Disagree somewhat	Agree somewhat	Strongly agree

12. The placement of taser (ECD) at a level IV (active resistance) on the resistance and response continuum is appropriate for most use of force incidents?

O	O	O	O	O
Strongly disagree	Uncertain	Disagree somewhat	Agree somewhat	Strongly agree

13. Based on your experience the policy change relating to placement of the taser (ECD) on the resistance and response continuum has decreased the number of times (frequency) that you have had to deploy your taser?

O	O	O	O	O
Strongly disagree	Uncertain	Disagree somewhat	Agree somewhat	Strongly agree

14. Based on your experience would you say that the change in agency policy relating to placement of the taser (ECD) on the resistance and response continuum has increased the changes that a suspect confrontation will escalate to deadly force?

O	O	O	O	O
Strongly disagree	Uncertain	Disagree somewhat	Agree somewhat	Strongly agree

15. Based on your experience would you say that the change in agency policy relating to placement of the taser (ECD) on the resistance and response continuum has increased the number of citizen's complaints related to taser deployments?

O	O	O	O	O
Strongly disagree	Uncertain	Disagree somewhat	Agree somewhat	Strongly agree

16. Based on your experience would you say that the change in agency policy relating to placement of the taser (ECD) on the resistance and response continuum makes you less inclined to verbally warn suspects prior to deploying the taser to gain compliance?

O	O	O	O	O
Strongly disagree	Uncertain	Disagree somewhat	Agree somewhat	Strongly agree

17. Based on your experience would you say that the change in agency policy relating to placement of the taser (ECD) on the resistance and response continuum makes you more inclined to other use of force options prior to deploying an ECD?

O	O	O	O	O
Strongly disagree	Uncertain	Disagree somewhat	Agree somewhat	Strongly agree

18. Based on your experience would you say that the change in agency policy relating to placement of the taser (ECD) on the resistance and response continuum decreases your ability to control suspects who are resistive or non compliant?

O	O	O	O	O
Strongly disagree	Uncertain	Disagree somewhat	Agree somewhat	Strongly agree

19. The main reason for the change in agency policy relating to placement of the taser (ECD) resistance and response continuum was to reduce citizen complaints?

O	O	O	O	O
Strongly disagree	Uncertain	Disagree somewhat	Agree somewhat	Strongly agree

20. The principal motivation for the change in agency policy relating to placement of the taser (ECD) on the resistance and response continuum was to reduce media scrutiny of taser (ECD) use?

O	O	O	O	O
Strongly disagree	Uncertain	Disagree somewhat	Agree somewhat	Strongly agree

21. The principal motivation for the change in agency policy relating to placement of the taser (ECD) on the resistance and response continuum was to reduce law suits related to taser (ECD) use?

O	O	O	O	O
Strongly disagree	Uncertain	Disagree somewhat	Agree somewhat	Strongly agree

22. Based on your experience would you say you have received adequate training on the deployment of tasers (ECD) after the policy change relating to placement of the taser (ECD) on the resistance and response continuum?

O	O	O	O	O
Strongly disagree	Uncertain	Disagree somewhat	Agree somewhat	Strongly agree

23. Based on your experience would you say that the use of tasers (ECD) on non compliant or resistive suspects causes more harm to suspects than the use of chemical agents?

O	O	O	O	O
Strongly disagree	Uncertain	Disagree somewhat	Agree somewhat	Strongly agree

24. Based on your experience would you say that the use of tasers (ECD) on non compliant or resistive suspects causes more harm to suspects than the use of a baton?

O	O	O	O	O
Strongly disagree	Uncertain	Disagree somewhat	Agree somewhat	Strongly agree

25. Based on your experience would you say that tasers (ECD) are more effective at incapacitating non compliant or resistive suspects than the use of a baton?

O	O	O	O	O
Strongly disagree	Uncertain	Disagree somewhat	Agree somewhat	Strongly agree

26. Based on your experience would you say that tasers (ECD) are more effective at incapacitating non compliant or resistive suspects than the use of Chemical Agents?

O	O	O	O	O
Strongly disagree	Uncertain	Disagree somewhat	Agree somewhat	Strongly agree

27. Based on your experience would you say that the placement of chemical agents at Level III (passive resistance) on the resistance and response continuum is appropriate for most use of force encounters?

O	O	O	O	O
Strongly disagree	Uncertain	Disagree somewhat	Agree somewhat	Strongly agree

28. Based on your experience would you say that the use of tasers (ECD) on non compliant or resistive suspects causes more harm to officers than the use of chemical agents?

O	O	O	O	O
Strongly disagree	Uncertain	Disagree somewhat	Agree somewhat	Strongly agree

29. Based on your experience would you say that being equipped with an (ECD) makes you safer when working as a police officer?

O	O	O	O	O
Strongly disagree	Uncertain	Disagree somewhat	Agree somewhat	Strongly agree

30. Based on your experience would you say that being equipped with an (ECD) makes you more confident in your ability to control non compliant or combative suspects?

O	O	O	O	O
Strongly disagree	Uncertain	Disagree somewhat	Agree somewhat	Strongly agree

31. Based on your experience would you say that the use of tasers (ECD) on non compliant or resistive suspects causes more harm to officers than the use of a baton?

O	O	O	O	O
Strongly disagree	Uncertain	Disagree somewhat	Agree somewhat	Strongly agree

32. Based on your experience would you say that the resistance and response continuum aids your decision making during a use of force encounter?

O	O	O	O	O
Strongly disagree	Uncertain	Disagree somewhat	Agree somewhat	Strongly agree

33. Based on your experience would you say that the resistance and response continuum makes your job as a police officer more dangerous?

O	O	O	O	O
Strongly disagree	Uncertain	Disagree somewhat	Agree somewhat	Strongly agree

34. Based on your experience and the recent increase in Orlando's violent crime would you say that the resistance and response continuum is appropriate for your current working environment?

O	O	O	O	O
Strongly disagree	Uncertain	Disagree somewhat	Agree somewhat	Strongly agree

4. General attitudinal questions about your job as a police officer

35. Enforcing the law is by far a patrol officer's most important responsibility.

O	O	O	O	O
Strongly disagree	Uncertain	Disagree somewhat	Agree somewhat	Strongly agree

36. A good patrol officer is one who patrols aggressively, stopping cars, checking out people, running license checks, and so forth.

O	O	O	O	O
Strongly disagree	Uncertain	Disagree somewhat	Agree somewhat	Strongly agree

37. Police officers have reason to be distrustful of most citizens?

  ○   ○   ○   ○   ○
 Strongly Uncertain Disagree Agree Strongly
 disagree   somewhat somewhat agree

38. My supervisors and managers understand my current working environment with regard to the use of force>

  ○   ○   ○   ○   ○
 Strongly Uncertain Disagree Agree Strongly
 disagree   somewhat somewhat agree

39. My supervisors and managers fairly evaluate my use of force decisions?

  ○   ○   ○   ○   ○
 Strongly Uncertain Disagree Agree Strongly
 disagree   somewhat somewhat agree

40. Most police officers use less force than they are authorized when dealing with non compliant or combative suspects?

  ○   ○   ○   ○   ○
 Strongly Uncertain Disagree Agree Strongly
 disagree   somewhat somewhat agree

References

Aberbach, J. and J. Walker. (1970) "Political Trust and Racial Ideology." *Political Science Review* 64 (1970): 1199-1219.

Adams, K, G. Alpert, R. Dunham, J. Garner, L. Greenfield, M. Henriquez, et al. *Use of force by police: Overview of national and local data.* Washington, DC: National Institute of Justice and Bureau of Justice Statistics, 1999.

Adams, K. and V. Jennison. "What We Do Not Know About Police Use of Tasers." *Policing: An International Journal of Police Strategies and Management* 30 (2007): 447-465.

Adang, O. and J. Mensink. "Pepper Spray: An Unreasonable Response to Suspect Verbal Resistance." *Policing: An International Journal of Police Strategies and Management* 24 (2004): 206-219.

Adkins, L. Oleoresin Capsicum: An Analysis of the Implementation of Pepper Spray into the Law Enforcement Use of Force Continuum in a Selected Police Department. (master's thesis, East Tennessee State University, 2003).

Aldrich, J. and F. Nelson . *Linear Probability, Logit and Probit Models.* Beverly Hills: Sage, 1985.

Alpert, G. and R. Dunham. *Policing Urban America* (3rd Edition). Prospect Heights: Illinois, 1997.

Alpert, G., R. Dunham, and J. MacDonald. (2004). "Interactive Police-Citizen Encounters That Result in Force." *Police Quarterly* 7, no. 4 (2004): 475-488.

Alpert, G. and J. MacDonald, J. "Police Use of Force: An Analysis of Organizational Characteristics." *Justice Quarterly* 18, no 2. (2001): 393-409.

Alpert, G. and M. Smith. "Police Use-of-Force Data: Where We Are and Where We Should Be Going." *Police Quarterly* 2 (1999): 57-78.

Alpert, G. and M. Smith. "Pepper Spray: A Safe and Reasonable Response to Suspect Verbal Resistance." *Policing: An International Journal of Police Strategies and Management* 23, no. 2 (2000): 50-68.

Amnesty International. (1997). "Recent Cases of the Use of Electroshock Weapons for Torture or Ill-Treatment." *Amnesty International.* 1997. http://www.amnestyusa.org/ annualreport.php?id=33E1D04C876F759C80256A2C0047B 07Eandc=USA (accessed August 26, 2007).

Amnesty International. (1999). "Cruelty in Control: The stun belt and other electroshock weapons in law enforcement." *Amnesty International.* 1999. www.amnestyusa.org/ rightsforall/stun/ cruelty/cruety-1.html (accessed June 24, 2006).

Amnesty International. (2004). "United States of America: Excessive and lethal force? Amnesty International's concerns about deaths and ill-treatment involving police use of tasers." *Amnesty International.* 2004. https://web. amnsety.org/library/index /ENGAMR511392004 (accessed June 24, 2006).

The Associated Press. (2008, January 17). "Forget Tupperware; It's taser party time." *The Associated Press.* 2008. http://www.msnbc.msn.com/id/22507292/print/1/displaymod e/1098/ (accessed January 17, 2008).

Auten, J. "The paramilitary model of police and police professionalism. In *The ambivalent force: Perspectives on the police* (3rd Edition) edited by A.S. Blumberg, and E.

Niederhoffer, 122-132. New York: Harcourt Brace College Publishers, 1985.

Babbie, E. *The Practice of Social Research* (9th Edition). Belmont, CA: Wadsworth, 2001.

Bailey, W. *Encyclopedia of Police Science* (2nd Edition). New York: Garland Press, 1995.

Bailey, W. "Less-than-lethal weapons and police citizen killings in U.S. urban areas." *Crime and Delinquency* 42 (1996): 535-552.

Bayley, D. and J. Garofalo. "The management of violence by police patrol officers." *Criminology* 27 (1989): 1-27.

Bayley, D. and H. Mendelsohn. *Minorities and the Police: Confrontation in America*. New York: Free Press, 1969.

Belotto, A. "Police (as victims of) brutality." *The Journal of California Law Enforcement* 35 (2001): 1-5.

Berenson, A. "As police use of tasers soars questions over safety emerge." *The New York Times*, July 18, 2004.

Berenson, A. "The safety of tasers is questioned again." *The New York Times*, May 25, 2006.

Bittner, E. *The functions of the police in modern society: A review of background factors, current practices, and possible role models*. Chevy Chase, MD: National Institute of Mental Health, Center for Studies of Crime and Delinquency, 1970.

Bittner, E. *Aspects of police work*. Boston: Northeastern University Press, 1990.

Bleetman, A. and R. Steyn. "The advanced taser: A medical review." *Taser*. 2003. http://www.taser.com/documents/ tasersubmit.pdf (accessed June 24, 2006).

Bohrnstedt, G. and T. Carter.. Robustness in Regression Analysis. *Sociological Methodology*, edited by J. Costner, 118-146. San Francisco: Jossey Bass, 1971.

Bowling, J. and M. Gaines. *Evaluation of oleoresin capsicum (O.C.) use by law enforcement agencies: Impact on injuries to officers and suspects, Final activity report.* Washington, DC: U.S. Department of Justice, NCJRS, 2000.

Bozeman, W., W. Hauda, J. Heck, D. Graham, B. Martin, B. and J. Winslow. "Safety and Injury profile of conducted electrical weapons used by law enforcement officers against criminal suspects." *Annals of Emergency Medicine* 53 (2009): 480-489.

Busemeyer, J. and L. Jones. "Analysis of Multiplicative Combination Rules When The Causal Variables are Measured with Error." *Psychological Bulletin* 93 (1983): 549-562.

Caplan, G. "Reflections on the nationalization of crime 1964-1968". *Arizona State University Law Journal* 3 (1973): 583-635.

Colarossi, A, J. Leusner, J, and K. Moore."Are OPD officers too quick to tase?" *Orlando Sentinel.* May 7, 2006. www.orlandosentinel. com/ news/local/orl-tasermain0706 may07,0,2347898.story (accessed on February 2, 2008).

Conner, G. "Use of force Continuum: Phase II." *Law and Order* 3 (1991): 30-32.

Cox, T., J. Faughn, and W. Nixon. "Police use of metal flashlights as weapons: An analysis of relevant problems." *Journal of Police Science and Administration* 13, no. 3 (1985): 244-250.

Crank, J. and R. Langworthy. "An Institutional Perspective of Policing." *The Journal* of *Criminal Law and Criminology* 83, no. 2 (1992): 338- 363.

Croft, E. "Police use of force: An empirical analysis." (doctoral dissertation, State University of New York at Albany, 1985).

Cronin J. and J. Ederheimer. *Conducted energy devices: Development of standards for consistency and guidance.* Washington, D.C: U.S. Department of Justice Office of Community Oriented Policing Services and Police Executive Research Forum, 2006.

Cusac, A. "Shock value: U.S. stun devices pose human rights risk." *The Progressive* 61 (1997): 28- 32.

Diedrich, J. "Police use new tasers frequently." *Milwaukee Journal Sentinel.* August 25, 2004.

DOMILL. Defense Scientific Advisory Council Subcommittee on the Medical Implications of less-lethal weapons. *Second Statement on the Medical Implications of the Use of the M26 Advanced TASER.* United Kingdom. July 27, 2004.

Ederheimer, J. and L. Fridell. *Chief concerns: Exploring the challenges of police use of force.* Washington, DC: Police Executive Research Forum, 2005.

Florida Department of Law Enforcement." Florida uniform crime report. County and municipal offense data, January – December 2005." Florida Department of Law Enforcement. http://www.fdle.state.fl.us/fsac/ucr/indx.asp (accessed November 28, 2007).

Florida Department of Law Enforcement. "2004 Criminal Justice Agency Profile: Statewide Ratios, Full-Time Officers per 1,000 Population." Florida Department of Law Enforcement. http://www.fdle.state.fl.us/cjst/CJAP/2004/ratio/ratio_totals. html (accessed April 2, 2008).

Florida Department of Law Enforcement. "Data and Statistics, UCR Offense Data: Total Index Crime for Florida by County, Jurisdiction and Offense, 2005". Florida Department of Law Enforcement. http://www.fdle.state.fl.us/fsac/data_ statistics.asp (accessed April 2, 2008).

Fish, R and L. Geddes. "Effects of Stun Guns and Tasers." *The Lancet* 358 (2001): 687-688.

Friedrich, R. "Police use of force: Individuals, situations, and organizations." *Annals of the American academy of political and social science* 452 (1980): 82-97.

Fyfe, J. "Administrative interventions in police shooting discretion: An empirical examination." *Journal of Criminal Justice* 7, no. 4 (1979): 309-323.

Fyfe, J. "The Metro-Dade police citizen violence reduction project: Summary of findings and recommendations." Paper presented at the annual meeting of the American Society of Criminology, Montreal, November 1987.

Fyfe, J. Police use of deadly force: Research and reform. *Justice Quarterly* 5 (1988): 165-207.

Fyfe, J., J. Greene, W. Walsh, O. Wilson, and R. McLaren, R. *Police Administration* (5th Edition). New York: McGraw-Hill, 1997.

Garner, J., T. Schrade, J. Hepburn, and J. Buchanan. "Measuring the continuum of force used by and against the police." *Criminal Justice Review* 20, no. 2 (1995): 146-168.

Garner, J., J. Buchanan, T. Schrade, and J. Hepburn. *Understanding the use of force by and against the police.* Washington, DC: National Institute of Justice, 1996.

Garner, J., C. Maxwell, C., and C. Heraux. "Characteristics associated with the prevalence and severity of force used by police." *Justice Quarterly* 19 (2002): 705-746.

Geller, W. and M. Scott. *Deadly force what we know.* Washington, DC: Police Executive Research Forum, 1992.

Geller, W. and H. Toch.. *And justice for all: A national agenda for understanding and controlling police use of force.* Washington, DC: Police Executive Research Forum, 1995.

Graham v. Connor. 409 U.S. 386, 109 S. Ct. 1865 (1989).

Greene. W. *Limdep Version 6.0: Users Manuel and Reference Guide*. Bellport, New York :Econometric Software, 1992.

Griffith, D. "Electrical storm: Human rights groups and the media implicated tasers in three recent deaths, but the autopsies told different stories." *Police* 6 (2002): 34-42.

Guyot, D. "Bending granite: Attempts to change the rank structure of American police departments." *Journal of Police Science and Administration* 7 (1979): 253-284.

Hamilton, A. (2002, February 4) "Stun guns for everyone: Are tasers the ultimate self defense tools or torture? A new model for consumers sparks debate." *Time Magazine,* February 4, 2002.

Holzworth, R. and C. Pipping, C. "Drawing a weapon: An analysis of police judgments." *Journal of Police Science Administration* 13 (1985): 185-194.

Homant, R. and D. Kennedy, D. "Effectiveness of less than lethal in suicide-by-cop incidents." *Police Quarterly,* 3 (2000): 53-171.

Hougland, S., C. Mesloh, and M. Henych. "Use of force, civil litigation, and the taser." *FBI Law Enforcement Bulletin* 74, no. 3 (2005): 24-30.

IACP. IACP National Law Enforcement Policy Center, Electronic control weapons: Concepts and issues paper, Alexandria Va., December 2004.

Jett, M. "Pepper Spray." *FBI Law Enforcement Bulletin* 66, no. 11 (1997): 17-24.

Kaminski, R., S. Edwards, and J. Johnson. "The deterrent effects of oleoresin capsicum on assaults against police: Testing the Velcro-effect hypothesis." *Police Quarterly* 1 (1998): 1-24.

Kaminski, R., S. Edwards, and J. Johnson, J. "Assessing the incapacitative effects of pepper spray during resistive encounters with the police." *Policing: An international journal of police strategies and management* 22 (1999): 7-29.

Kavanagh, J. "The occurrence of revisiting arrest in arrest encounters: A study of police-citizen violence." *Criminal Justice Review* 22 (1997): 16-33.

Kelling, G. and M. Wycoff. M. "Evolving strategy of policing: Case studies of strategic change." 2001. http://www.ncjrs. gov/pdffiles1/ nij/grants/198029.pdf (accessed June 24, 2006).

Kennedy, P. *A Guide to Econometrics.* Cambridge, MA: MIT Press, 1992.

King, W. "Bending granite revisited: The command rank structure of American police organizations." *Policing: An international journal of police strategies and management* 26 (2003): 208-222.

Klinger, D. "The micro-structure of non-lethal force: Baseline data from an observational study." *Criminal Justice Review* 20, no. 2 (1995): 169-186.

Klockars, C. (1996). A theory of excessive force and its control. In *Police Violence*, edited by W. Gellar and H. Toch, 1-19. New Haven, CT: Yale University Press, 1969.

Kornblum, R. and S. Reddy. "The effects of the TASER in fatalities involving police confrontation." *Journal of Forensic Sciences* 36 (1991): 434-448.

Lamb, C. Nonlethal weapons policy. Department of Defense Directive, January 1995.

Langan, P., L. Greenfield, S. Smith, M. Durose, M., and D. Levin. *Contacts between police and the public: Findings from the 1999 national survey.* Washington, DC: Bureau of Justice Statistics, 2001.

Lersch, K. and T. Mieczkowski. "Violent Police Behavior: Past, present, and future research directions." *Aggression and*

Violent Behavior: A review journal 10, no. 5 (2006), 552-568.

Lewer, N. 'Non-lethal weapons: Operational and policy developments." *The Lancet Extreme Medicine* 362 (2003): 20-21.

Lewer, N. and N. Davison. Bradford non-lethal weapons research project. Research Report 8, Centre for conflict resolution department of peace studies, 2006.

Lingamneni, J. "Resistance to Change in Police Organizations: The Diffusion Paradigm." *Criminal Justice Review* 4, no. 2 (1979), 17-26.

Lundstrom, R. and C. Mullan. "The use of force: One department's experience." *FBI Law Enforcement Bulletin* (January 1987): 6-9.

Lumb, R. and P. Friday. "Impact of pepper spray availability on police officer use-of-force decisions." *Policing: An international journal of police strategy and management* 20 (1997): 136-148.

Manning, P. "Information technologies and the police." In *Modern Policing*, edited by M. Tonry and N. Morris, 349-398. Chicago: University of Chicago Press, 1992.

Manning, P. "The study of policing." *Police Quarterly* 8, no. 1 (2005), 23-43.

Marks, P. "The shocking use of police stun guns." *New Scientist* 188 (2005): 30-31.

McBride, D. and N. Tedder, N. *Efficacy and safety of electrical stun weapons.* Washington DC: Potomac Institute for Policy Studies, 2005.

McCluskey, J. and W. Terrill. "Departmental and citizen complaints as predictors of police coercion." *Policing: An international journal of police strategy and management* 28 (2005): 513-529.

McEwen, T. and F. Leahy, F. *Less than lethal technologies in law enforcement and correctional agencies.* Washington, DC: Institute for Law and Justice, Bureau of Justice Statistics, 1993.

McEwen, T. "Policies on less than lethal force in law enforcement agencies." *Policing: An international journal of police strategy and management* 20 (1997): 39-59.

McLaughlin, V. *Police and the use of force: The Savannah study.* Westport, CT: Praeger, 1992.

McManus, J., T. Forsyth, R. Hawks, R., and J. Jui. "A respective case series describing the injury pattern of the advanced M26 TASER in Multnomah County, Oregon." *Academic Emergency Medicine* 11 (2004): 587.

Menard, Scott. *Applied Logistic Regression Analysis.* Thousand Oaks, CA: Sage, 1995.

Meyer, G. "Non-lethal weapons vs. conventional police tactics: Assessing injuries and liabilities." *The Police Chief,* 8 (1992): 10-18.

Miller, N. "Less than lethal force weaponry law enforcement and correctional agency civil law liability for the use of excessive force." *Creighton Law Review,* 28 (1995): 733-794.

Mosher, F. *Government reorganizations: Cases and commentary.* New York: Bobbs Merrill, 1967.

Morabito E. and Doerner, W. "Police use of less than lethal force: Oleoresin capsicum (OC) spray." *Policing: An international journal of police strategy and management* 20 (1997): 680-697.

National Institute of Justice. *The evolution and development of police technology.* Washington, DC: National Institute of Justice, 1998.

National Institute of Justice. *Study of Deaths Following Electro Muscular Disruption: Interim Report.* Washington, DC: National Institute of Justice, 2008.

Nielson, E. "The advanced TASER: TASER International takes the TASER to a higher level." *Law and Order* 49 (2001): 57-62.

Norušis, M. *SPSS 14.0 Statistical Procedures Companion.* Upper Saddle River, NJ: Prentice Hall, 2005.

OCSO Taser Task Force. *Orange County Sheriff's Office Taser Task Force Final Report.* March 4, 2005.

Ordog, G., J. Wasserberger, T. Schalater, and S. Balasubramanium. "Electronic gun (TASER) injuries." *Annals of Emergency Medicine,* 16 (1987): 73-78.

Parent, R. "Police shootings: Reducing the risks." *Law and Order* (2000): 82-84.

Peak, K. "The quest for alternatives to lethal force: A heuristic view." *Journal of Contemporary Criminal Justice* 6 (1990): 8-22.

Pilant, L. "Less-than-lethal weapons: New solutions for law enforcement." *Science and Technology*, International Association of Chiefs of Police, December 1993.

Police Executive Research Forum. (2005). "PERF conducted energy devices and training guidelines for consideration." Retrieved on June 24, 2006 from www.policeforum.org

President's Commission on Law Enforcement and Administration of Justice. *The Challenge of Crime in a Free Society,* Washington, DC: U.S. Government Printing Office, 1967.

Razor, C. "Is it time to change law enforcement's paramilitary structure?" in *Controversial Issues in Policing*, edited by J.D. Sewell, J.D., 139-153. Boston: Allyn and Bacon, 1999.

Ready, J., M. White, M. and C. Fisher. "Shock Value: A comparative analysis of news reports and official police records on taser deployments." *Policing,* 31 (2008): 148-170.

Reiss, A. *The police and the public.* New Haven, CT: Yale University Press, 1971.

Riksheim, E. and S. Chermak, S. "Causes of police behavior revisited." *Journal of Criminal Justice* 21 (1993): 353-382.

Robin, G. "The illusive and illuminating search for less than lethal alternatives to deadly force." *Police Forum* 6, no. 2 (1996): 1-20.

Schroeder, L., D. Sjoquist, and P. Stephan. *Understanding Regression Analysis: An Introductory Guide.* Beverly Hills: Sage Publications, 1986.

Sherman, L. and M. Blumberg. "Higher education and police use of deadly force." *Journal of Criminal Justice* 9 (1981): 317-331.

Smith, D. "The neighborhood context of police behavior." In *Communities and Crime,* edited by A.J. Reiss Jr. and M. Tonry, 313-341. Chicago: University of Chicago Press, 1986.

Smith, M. and M. Petrocelli, M. "The effectiveness of force used by police in making arrests." *Police Practice and Research* 3 (2002): 201-215.

Smith, M., M. Petrocelli, and C. Sheer. "Excessive force, civil liability, and the Taser in the nation's courts: Implications for law enforcement policy and practice." *Policing: An International Journal of Police Strategies and Management* 30 (2006): 398-422.

SPD. Seattle Police Department Special Report Taser Implementation, Year 1, May 2002.

Stetser, M. *The use of force in police control of violence: Incidents resulting in assaults on officers.* New York: LFB Scholarly Publishing, 2001.

Stewart, J. "Value conflict and policy change." *The Review of Policy Research.* 23 (2006): 183-96.

Strote, J. and H. Hutson. "Taser Use in Restraint-Related Deaths." *Prehospital Emergency Care,* 10 (2006): 447-450.

Sturman, M. (1996). *Multiple approaches to absenteeism analysis* (CAHRS Working Paper #96-07). Ithaca, NY: Cornell University, School of Industrial and Labor Relations, Center for Advanced Human Resource Studies. http://digitalcommons.ilr.cornell.edu/ cahrswp/178 (accessed April 15, 2008).

Sykes, R. and E. Brent. "The regulation of interaction by police." *Criminology* 18 (1980):182-197.

Tabachnick, B and L. Fidell. *Using Multivariate Statistics* (3rd Edition). New York: Harper Collins, 1996.

Taser International Inc. (2004) Press Releases. July 2004, http://www.TASER.com/press releases (accessed July 24, 2006).

Tennessee v. Garner. (1985). 471 U.S. 1, 8-9.

Terrill, W. *Police coercion: Application of the force continuum.* Publishing: New York: LFB Scholarly Publishing, 2001.

Terrill, W. "Police use of force and suspect resistance: The micro process of the police-suspect encounter." *Police Quarterly* 6 (2003): 51-83.

Terrill, W. "Police use of force: A transactional approach." *Justice Quarterly,* 22 (2005): 107-138.

Terrill, W., G. Alpert, R. Dunham, and M. Smith. "A management tool for evaluating police use of force: An application of the force factor." *Police Quarterly* 6 (2003): 150-171.

Terrill, W. and S. Mastrofski. "Situational and officer based determinants of police coercion." *Justice Quarterly* 19 (2002): 215-248.

Terrill, W. and E. Paoline, E. "Force Continuums: Moving beyond speculation and toward empiricism" [Electronic Version]. *Law Enforcement Executive Forum* 7 (2007).

Thacher, D. and M. Rein. "Managing value conflict in public policy." *Governance: An international journal of policy, administration, and institutions* 17 (2004): 457-486.

Truncale, J. "Batons: A short history." *The Journal* 3 (1996): 44-122.

United States Department of Defense. Human Effects Center for Excellence, Report on Human Effectiveness and Risk Characterization for Electro Muscular Incapacitation Devices, 2004.

United States Department of Justice. "Bureau of Justice Statistics: Law Enforcement Management and Administrative Statistics (LEMAS), Local Police Departments." 2003. http://www.ojp.usdoj.gov/bjs/abstract/ lpd03.htm (accessed April 2, 2008).

United States Government Accountability Office. "Report to the Chairman, Subcommittee on National Security, Emerging Threats and International Relations, Committee on Government Reform, House of Representatives: TASER Weapons Use of Taser weapons by selected Law Enforcement Agencies." May 2005.

Vila, B. and C. Morris. *The role of police in American society: A documentary history.* Westport, CT: Greenwood Press, 1999.

Vogel, K. Tasertron tactics. *Law and Order* 46 (1998): 49-52.

Wadman, R. and W. Allison. *To protect and serve: A history of police in America.* Upper Saddle River, New Jersey: , 2004.

Walker, S. *The Police in America: An introduction*, (3rd Edition). Boston: McGraw-Hill, 1999.

Weaver, W. and M. Jett. *Oleoresin capsicum training and use.* Quantico, Virginia: FBI Academy Firearms Training Unit, 1989.

Weisburd, D. *Statistics in Criminal Justice.* Belmont, CA: West/Wadsworth, 1998.

White, M. and J. Ready, J. "The Taser as a Less Lethal Force Alternative: Findings on Use and Effectiveness in a Large Metropolitan Police Agency." *Police Quarterly* 10 (2007): 170-191.

Wilkening, D. "Tasers under fire." *Police Department Disciplinary Bulletin* 13, no. 6 (2005), 1-2.

Williams, H. *Taser Electronic Control Devices and Sudden In-Custody Death: Separating Evidence from Conjecture.* Springfield, IL: Charles C. Thomas, 2008.

Williams, G. and R. Simon. "Tasertron's 95HP: The law enforcement taser." *Law and Order* 49 (2001): 80-83.

Worden, R. "The causes of police brutality: Theory and evidence on police use of force." In *And Justice for all: Understanding and controlling police abuse of force*, edited by W. Geller and H. Toch, 31-60. Washington, DC: Police Executive Research Forum, 1995.

Index

rec. apr. 12, 2011